luscious fruit desserts

The Editors of
Williams-Sonoma

photographs by
John Lee

weldon**owen**

contents

year-round baking

Seasonally organized, this book features more than 50 recipes, each one crafted to take advantage of fruit at the pinnacle of freshness. Fruit is a perfect end to many meals, and the dry heat of an oven intensifies fruits' inherent flavors while caramelizing their natural sugars. Most fruit desserts, including the ones inside this book, offer the benefit of being easy to make, good examples of the culinary principle that if you start with the finest ingredients and prepare them in ways that highlight their natural qualities, you'll get outstanding results.

spring

Spring is a transitional season, and you'll find different fruits in the market depending on the climate in which you live. In the early spring, you will still find winter's citrus fruits in the bins. As the weather warms, early raspberries and apricots start to make an appearance. Rhubarb's bright red stalks push up through the soil at the first sign of warmth. And strawberries are a sure sign that spring is in full swing.

summer

As the weather warms, the abundance of berries—raspberries, strawberries, blueberries, and blackberries with all their kin—reaches full tilt. Stone fruits, too—peaches, plums, nectarines, and others—proliferate in farmers' markets as well as roadside fruit stands, lingering into early fall. Cherries, both sweet and sour varieties, come into their own in the hot weather, and their short season calls for snapping them up as soon as you can.

fall

Cooling weather means that late-ripening tree fruits—pears, apples, and quinces—take over where stone fruits left off. Fall is when figs really come into their own, turning plump, juicy, and begging to be eaten. Pumpkins are one of the most popular ingredients for desserts this time of year, and grapes are at their peak. Cranberries show up just in time for Thanksgiving baking and linger as we approach the end of the year.

winter

The winter season brings inclement weather, and local fruit harvests can be spotty. Still, apples, pears, and citrus fruits thrive and can be baked into sweet, comforting treats. Tropical fruits like bananas and pineapples, shipped in from exotic locations, add a bright boost to dreary days. Persimmons, pumpkins, and cranberries add their iconic flavors to sweet treats baked during the festive holiday party season.

spring

raspberry-buttermilk sheet cake

MAKES 12 SERVINGS

1 cup (8 oz/250 g) unsalted butter, at room temperature, plus butter for greasing

2½ cups (12½ oz/390 g) all-purpose flour

½ teaspoon baking powder

¼ teaspoon baking soda

¼ teaspoon salt

1¼ cups (10 oz/315 g) granulated sugar

3 large eggs, at room temperature

1 cup (8 fl oz/250 ml) buttermilk, at room temperature

12 oz (375 g) fresh raspberries (about 4 cups)

Confectioners' sugar for dusting (optional)

We like this cake as is, sprinkled with confectioners' sugar and cut into squares. Or, you can cut the cake in half crosswise, stack the halves, and layer buttercream (page 32) between the layers. You can also bake the batter in a buttered 9-by-13-inch (23-by-33-cm) pan, which will yield a thicker cake. Add 10–15 minutes to the baking time.

1 Preheat the oven to 325°F (165°C). Butter a half sheet pan (13-by-18 inches/33 by 45 cm) and line it with parchment paper.

2 In a bowl, whisk together the flour, baking powder, baking soda, and salt; set aside.

3 Using an electric mixer, beat together the butter and granulated sugar on medium speed until smooth, 3–5 minutes. Add the eggs 1 at a time, beating well after each addition and scraping down the bowl as needed. Add the buttermilk and beat until combined. Add the flour mixture and beat just until blended.

4 Pour the batter into the prepared pan and spread evenly. Scatter the raspberries on top, gently pressing them down into the batter.

5 Bake until golden brown and a tester inserted into the center of the cake comes out clean, 20–25 minutes. Let cool completely on a wire rack, about 1 hour. If desired, dust lightly with confectioners' sugar just before serving.

strawberry tart with orange cream

MAKES 8 SERVINGS

Basic Tart Dough (page 120)

½ lb (250 g) full-fat cream cheese, at room temperature

¼ cup (2 oz/60 g) sugar

1 teaspoon finely grated orange zest

2 teaspoons orange liqueur

½ lb (250 g) fresh strawberries (about 2 cups), hulled and halved lengthwise

½ cup (5 oz/155 g) apricot jam

This elegant, make-ahead tart is the perfect dessert for a dinner party. It looks like it is difficult to put together but is actually very easy. Full-fat cream cheese will yield the best results, although reduced fat will also work; do not use nonfat cream cheese for this recipe.

1 On a lightly floured surface, roll out the dough into a 12-inch (30-cm) round about ⅛ inch (3 mm) thick. Transfer it to a 9½-inch (24-cm) tart pan, preferably with a removable bottom, and fit the dough into the pan (see page 117). Trim off any excess by gently running a rolling pin across the top of the pan. Press the dough into the sides of the pan so that it extends slightly above the rim. Refrigerate or freeze the tart shell until firm, about 30 minutes.

2 Meanwhile, place a rack in the lower third of the oven and preheat to 400°F (200°C). Fully bake the tart shell (see page 122). Let the tart shell cool completely on a wire rack, about 30 minutes.

3 Using an electric mixer, beat together the cream cheese and sugar on medium speed until smooth, 3–5 minutes. Beat in the orange zest and liqueur until combined. Spread

the cream cheese mixture evenly over the bottom of the tart shell. Arrange the strawberry halves in concentric circles on top, completely covering the surface of the tart.

4 In a small saucepan, warm the apricot jam over low heat until it liquefies. Pour through a fine-mesh sieve set over a small bowl to strain out any fruit chunks. Using a small pastry brush, gently brush the strawberries with a thin coating of the jam to glaze the fruit. Refrigerate until ready to serve, at least 1 hour and up to 24 hours.

5 Let the tart stand at room temperature for about 20 minutes before serving. If using a tart pan with a removable bottom, let the sides fall away, then slide the tart onto a serving plate.

strawberry-rhubarb brown betty

MAKES 8 SERVINGS

½ cup (4 oz/125 g) unsalted butter, melted and cooled, plus butter for greasing

2 cups (4 oz/125 g) fine fresh bread crumbs

1 cup (7 oz/220 g) firmly packed light brown sugar

½ teaspoon ground nutmeg

2½ cups (12 oz/375 g) thinly sliced rhubarb

1½ lb (750 g) fresh strawberries (about 6 cups), hulled and sliced

A brown betty is one of the easiest fruit desserts to throw together. You don't need to make a separate dough, which keeps prep time manageable. Instead, sweetened, buttered bread crumbs are layered with fresh fruit and then baked for a simple, homey, but irresistible dessert.

1 Preheat the oven to 375°F (190°C). Lightly butter a 2½-qt (2.5-l) shallow baking dish.

2 In a bowl, using a fork, stir together the bread crumbs and brown sugar. Add the nutmeg and melted butter and stir until the ingredients are evenly moistened. In another bowl, stir together the rhubarb and strawberries.

3 Sprinkle half of the crumb mixture in the bottom of the prepared baking dish. Spread the fruit mixture evenly over the top, then sprinkle with the remaining crumb mixture.

4 Bake until the top is golden and the fruit is bubbling, about 45 minutes. Let cool on a wire rack for 15 minutes before serving, or let cool completely and serve at room temperature.

strawberry-rhubarb coffee cake

MAKES 8–10 SERVINGS

Unsalted butter for greasing

For the Topping
2 tablespoons sugar
½ teaspoon ground cinnamon

For the Cake
4 large eggs, at room temperature
1⅓ cups (11 oz/345 g) sugar
¾ cup (6 fl oz/180 ml) canola oil
3 cups (15 oz/470 g) all-purpose flour
2 teaspoons baking soda
1 teaspoon baking powder
1 teaspoon salt
2 teaspoons ground cinnamon
1 lb (500 g) fresh strawberries (about 4 cups), hulled and coarsely chopped
¼ lb (125 g) rhubarb stalks, cut into ½-inch (12-mm) slices

Fresh rhubarb is sold in long, red or pale pink stalks in the late spring and early summer. Be sure to remove any leaves from the stalks, which are inedible. Rhubarb and strawberries are a popular combination. We like the duo baked in this simple cinnamon-scented coffee cake.

1 Preheat the oven to 350°F (180°C). Butter a 9-inch (23-cm) angel food cake pan with a removable bottom.

2 To make the topping, in a small bowl, stir together the sugar and cinnamon. Set aside.

3 To make the cake, using an electric mixer, beat together the eggs and sugar on medium-high speed for about 1 minute. Increase the speed to high, add the oil, and beat until thick and pale, about 2 minutes.

4 In another bowl, whisk together the flour, baking soda, baking powder, salt, and cinnamon. Add the flour mixture to the egg mixture and, using the mixer on low speed or a wooden spoon, beat until thoroughly blended, about 1 minute. Add the strawberries (and their juice, if any) and rhubarb. Using a large rubber spatula, gently fold the berries into the batter just until evenly distributed. Take care not to break up the fruit. Do not overmix. Pour the batter into the prepared pan and spread evenly. Sprinkle with the topping.

5 Bake until the top is golden brown and a tester inserted into the center of the cake comes out clean, 60–70 minutes. Run a knife between the cake and the sides of the pan, and lift up the center tube to separate the cake from the pan sides. Let cool completely on a wire rack, about 1 hour.

6 Run a knife under the bottom and around the sides of the tube, invert the cake to remove the tube, and place the cake upright on a serving plate.

raspberry cream scones

MAKES 8-10 SCONES

2⅓ cups (11½ oz/360 g) all-purpose flour

1 tablespoon baking powder

½ teaspoon salt

⅓ cup (3 oz/90 g) granulated sugar

½ cup (4 oz/125 g) cold unsalted butter, cut into small pieces

⅔ cup (5 fl oz/160 ml) plus 3 tablespoons heavy cream, at room temperature

1 large egg yolk, lightly beaten, at room temperature

1 container (6 oz/185 g) fresh raspberries

½ cup (2 oz/60 g) confectioners' sugar

Flaky with layers of butter and rich with cream, these scones are truly decadent. Serve warm for breakfast or at room temperature for an afternoon tea. You can use almost any type of soft, fresh fruit, but fresh raspberries give nice hits of tartness to the scones. They're best when eaten the same day they're baked.

1 Preheat the oven to 375°F (190°C). Line a rimmed baking sheet with parchment paper.

2 Using an electric mixer, briefly beat together the flour, baking powder, salt, and granulated sugar. Add the butter and beat on medium speed until pea-sized pieces form, about 4 minutes. Add the ⅔ cup (5 fl oz/160 ml) cream and the egg yolk and beat until the dough just starts to come together (you want it to be a little shaggy).

3 Turn the dough out onto a lightly floured work surface. Scatter two-thirds of the raspberries on top. Gather and press the dough to form a flat rectangle. Fold it from the short ends into the center to form a square, pressing down gently (it should still be slightly shaggy and a few berries will be loose).

Scatter the remaining raspberries on top and fold again, pressing them into the dough. Gather any pieces that have fallen off. The dough will be very wet. Tear off small, evenly sized handfuls of dough and place on the prepared baking sheet about 2 inches (5 cm) apart. You should have 8–10 scones, depending on the size.

4 Bake until golden brown, about 20 minutes, rotating the baking sheet halfway through baking. Let the scones cool directly on a wire rack for about 15 minutes.

5 When the scones are almost cool, in a small bowl, whisk together the 3 tablespoons cream and the confectioners' sugar. Drizzle the icing over the scones.

rhubarb-berry pie

MAKES 8 SERVINGS

**Double recipe Basic
Pie Dough (page 120),
divided into 2 disks**

**1 cup (8 oz/250 g) sugar,
plus more for sprinkling**

3 tablespoons cornstarch

¼ teaspoon salt

**1¼ lb (625 g) rhubarb stalks,
cut into ½-inch (12-mm) slices**

**1 container (6 oz/185 g)
fresh raspberries**

**2 tablespoons unsalted butter,
cut into small pieces**

**1 large egg beaten with
1 tablespoon heavy cream**

Rhubarb tends to be very tart, so we like to pair it with a sweet fruit and a little sugar to balance its flavor. To lend the double-crust pie additional charm, you can cut shapes into the top crust with a small cookie cutter before placing it on top of the pie, or keep it simple by cutting a couple of slits into the top crust with a knife.

1 Preheat the oven to 425°F (220°C). Have ready a 9-inch (23-cm) pie dish or pan.

2 On a lightly floured surface, roll out 1 dough disk into a 12-inch (30-cm) round about ⅛ inch (3 mm) thick. Transfer to the pie dish and fit the dough into the pan (see page 117). Roll out the other dough disk for the top crust into the same-sized round.

3 In a large bowl, stir together the sugar, cornstarch, and salt. Add the rhubarb and raspberries and stir to mix well. Pour the filling into the crust and spread evenly. Dot with the butter.

Place the top crust over the filling and trim the edges, leaving a ¾-inch (2-cm) overhang. Fold the overhang under itself and crimp decoratively (see page 118). Cut a few steam vents in the top crust. Gently brush the crust with the egg mixture, then sprinkle with sugar.

4 Bake for 20 minutes. Reduce the oven temperature to 350°F (180°C) and continue to bake until the juices are bubbling and the crust is browned, 30–40 minutes longer, covering the edges with aluminum foil if the crust browns too quickly. Let cool on a wire rack for about 2 hours before serving.

raspberry gratin

MAKES 6–8 SERVINGS

3 large egg yolks

½ cup (4 oz/125 g) sugar

½ cup (4 fl oz/125 ml) framboise liqueur

2 cups (16 fl oz/500 ml) cold heavy cream

1½ lb (750 g) fresh raspberries (about 6 cups)

Depending on the year and the climate in which you live, raspberries come to market at different times. Start looking for them in late spring when the weather begins to warm. This dessert showcases the sweet fruits at their best. A simple egg custard is lightened with whipped cream, then the mixture is spooned over the berries and placed briefly under the broiler.

1 In the top pan of a double boiler or in a heatproof metal bowl, combine the egg yolks, sugar, and 1 tablespoon water. Place over (not touching) barely simmering water and heat, whisking constantly, until the mixture is foamy and begins to thicken slightly, 2–3 minutes. Immediately remove from the heat and strain into a bowl. Stir in the framboise, cover, and refrigerate for at least 4 hours or up to overnight.

2 Just before serving, position the oven rack 3–4 inches (7.5–10 cm) from the heat source in a broiler and preheat the broiler.

3 Using an electric mixer, whip the cream on medium-high speed until soft peaks form, about 2 minutes. Using a rubber spatula, gently fold the cream into the chilled egg mixture. Scatter the berries over the bottom of a 2-qt (2-l) baking dish. Place on a rimmed baking sheet. Gently pour and spoon the lightened egg mixture over the berries.

4 Broil until the top is browned and bubbling, 1½–2 minutes. Let cool for about 2 minutes, then serve right away.

apricot–brown sugar crumble

MAKES 8 SERVINGS

Unsalted butter for greasing

For the Topping
¾ cup (4 oz/125 g)
all-purpose flour

¾ cup (6 oz/185 g) firmly
packed golden brown sugar

½ teaspoon salt

¼ teaspoon ground cinnamon

½ cup (4 oz/125 g) unsalted
butter, at room temperature,
cut into chunks

For the Filling
2 lb (1 kg) apricots, pitted
and cut into chunks

2 teaspoons fresh
lemon juice

½ teaspoon vanilla extract

2 tablespoons
all-purpose flour

⅓ cup (3 oz/90 g)
granulated sugar

Too busy to make a pie? Try a crumble. It has all the same flavors, but there's no need to mess with a crust: just spoon the fruit into a baking dish and scatter with the simple crumbly topping. This crumble is delicious on its own, or serve portions with scoops of vanilla ice cream. In the summer, swap in other types of stone fruits, if you like.

1 Preheat the oven to 400°F (200°C). Butter a 9-inch (23-cm) pie dish.

2 To make the topping, in a bowl, stir together the flour, brown sugar, salt, and cinnamon. Scatter the butter over the flour mixture and, using a pastry blender or 2 knives, cut in the butter until it is evenly distributed and the mixture begins to form clumps.

3 To make the filling, in a large bowl, stir together the apricots, lemon juice, and vanilla. Add the flour and granulated sugar and toss again to coat the fruit evenly. Transfer to the prepared baking dish and sprinkle the topping evenly over the fruit.

4 Bake until the fruit is bubbling and the topping is golden, about 40 minutes. Let cool on a wire rack for about 20 minutes. Serve warm.

roasted strawberry sundaes

MAKES 6–8 SERVINGS

2 pints (16 oz/500 g)
strawberries

2 tablespoons melted butter

1 tablespoon sugar

Freshly ground black pepper

2 tablespoons aged
balsamic vinegar

1 pt (14 oz/440 g) vanilla
ice cream

Roasting strawberries really intensifies their natural sweetness, and sweet-tart balsamic vinegar and black pepper lend contrasting flavors to excite your palate. Spoon the warm fruit mixture over scoops of vanilla ice cream for easy sundaes, Italian style.

1 Preheat the oven to 400°F (200°C). While the oven heats, hull the strawberries and halve them lengthwise.

2 Spread the strawberries on a rimmed baking sheet. Drizzle with the melted butter and sprinkle with the sugar and a few grinds of pepper. Toss to coat the berries evenly, then spread them out in a single layer on the baking sheet. Roast until the berries are softened, about 10 minutes.

3 When the berries are done, transfer them to a bowl. Add the balsamic vinegar and toss gently. Let the berries cool for 5 minutes. Meanwhile, let the ice cream stand at room temperature to soften slightly.

4 Divide the ice cream among bowls, top with the strawberry mixture, dividing evenly, and serve right away.

strawberry-citrus muffins

MAKES 16 MUFFINS

2¼ cups (11½ oz/360 g) all-purpose flour

2 teaspoons baking powder

1 teaspoon baking soda

½ teaspoon salt

¾ cup (6 oz/185 g) sugar

½ cup (4 fl oz/125 ml) milk, at room temperature

½ cup (4 oz/125 g) sour cream, at room temperature

⅓ cup (3 fl oz/80 ml) canola oil

1 large egg, at room temperature

1 tablespoon grated orange zest

1 cup (4 oz/125 g) hulled and thinly sliced fresh strawberries, patted dry

About ⅓ cup (4 oz/125 g) strawberry jam

Laced with strawberry slices, strawberry jam, and orange zest, these muffins are perfect to serve at a spring brunch. Sour cream in the batter makes them moist and tangy. To keep the strawberry juices from coloring the batter, pat the berries dry after slicing.

1 Preheat the oven to 400°F (200°C). Line 16 standard muffin cups with paper liners; fill any unused cups one-third full with water.

2 In a large bowl, whisk together the flour, baking powder, baking soda, and salt; set aside.

3 In a bowl, whisk together the sugar, milk, sour cream, oil, egg, and orange zest until smooth, then stir in the strawberries. Add the milk mixture to the flour mixture and stir just until blended. Do not overmix.

4 Place a spoonful of batter in each prepared muffin cup. Add a scant 1 teaspoon strawberry jam to each cup, then spoon the remaining batter on top, filling each cup about two-thirds full.

5 Bake until a tester inserted into the center of a muffin comes out clean, 15–18 minutes. Let the muffins cool in the pans on wire racks for 5 minutes. Turn the muffins out of the pan and serve warm or at room temperature.

gingered rhubarb crisp

MAKES 8 SERVINGS

1½ lb (750 g) rhubarb stalks,
cut into ¼-inch (6-mm) slices

3 oranges

1 cup (8 oz/250 g)
granulated sugar

3-inch (7.5-cm) piece fresh
ginger, peeled and grated

1½ cups (7½ oz/235 g)
all-purpose flour

¾ cup (6 oz/185 g) firmly
packed light brown sugar

½ cup (1½ oz/45 g)
quick-cooking rolled oats

½ teaspoon ground cinnamon

¼ teaspoon salt

6 tablespoons (3 oz/90 g)
unsalted butter, melted
and cooled

Vanilla ice cream
for serving

Fresh ginger adds a warm, spicy bite to this classic crisp with a crunchy oat topping. We like to serve this comforting dessert on a rainy spring evening topped with vanilla ice cream. As the ice cream melts onto the warm crisp, it offers a nice contrast in temperature and texture.

1 Preheat the oven to 375°F (190°C). Have ready a 9-by-13-inch (23-by-33-cm) baking dish.

2 Place the rhubarb in the baking dish. Finely grate the zest from one of the oranges and add it to the dish. Squeeze ⅔ cup (5 fl oz/160 ml) juice from the remaining oranges and add it to the dish along with the granulated sugar. Toss the rhubarb mixture well, then spread it out evenly in the dish.

3 In a bowl, using a fork, stir together the ginger, flour, brown sugar, oats, cinnamon, and salt. Add the melted butter and stir until the ingredients are evenly moistened. Sprinkle the oat mixture evenly over the rhubarb. Bake for 15 minutes.

4 Loosely cover the baking dish with aluminum foil and continue to bake until the topping is browned and the juices are thick and bubbling around the edges, 15–20 minutes longer. Let cool, uncovered, on a wire rack for at least 20 minutes.

5 To serve, spoon the warm crisp into bowls, top with scoops of ice cream, and serve right away.

white chocolate–raspberry cupcakes

For the Cupcakes

2 cups (10 oz/315 g) all-purpose flour

2 teaspoons baking powder

¼ teaspoon salt

½ cup (4 oz/125 g) unsalted butter, at room temperature

1 cup (8 oz/250 g) sugar

3 large egg whites, at room temperature

½ cup (4 fl oz/125 ml) whole milk, at room temperature

2 oz (60 g) white chocolate, chopped and melted (page 123)

1 container (6 oz/185 g) fresh raspberries

For the Buttercream

3 large egg whites, at room temperature

Pinch of salt

⅔ cup (5 oz/155 g) sugar

1 cup (8 oz/250 g) very soft unsalted butter

2 tablespoons smashed and strained raspberries

Chunk of white chocolate for shaving

Sweet white chocolate and tart raspberries are always a winning combination. Choose good-quality white chocolate that comes in a bar or block for this recipe, since the chips from a bag don't melt well or blend into batters.

1 Preheat the oven to 350°F (180°C). Line 12 standard muffin cups with paper liners.

2 To make the cupcakes, in a large bowl, whisk together the flour, baking powder, and salt.

3 Using an electric mixer, beat together the butter and sugar on medium speed until light and fluffy, 3–5 minutes. Add the egg whites and beat until blended, scraping down the bowl as needed. Add the flour mixture in 3 additions alternately with the milk in 2 additions, starting and ending with the flour mixture. Beat just until combined. Stir in the white chocolate just until blended, then gently fold in the raspberries. Spoon the batter into the prepared muffin cups, dividing evenly.

4 Bake until the cupcakes are puffed and light golden and the center springs back slightly when touched, about 25 minutes. Let cool completely on a wire rack, about 30 minutes.

5 To make the buttercream, in a metal bowl of a stand mixer, using a handheld whisk, whisk together the egg whites, salt, and sugar. Place over (not touching) barely simmering water in a large saucepan and heat, whisking constantly, until the sugar dissolves and the mixture is warm to the touch, 3–5 minutes. Remove from the heat.

6 Put the bowl on the mixer and, using the whisk attachment, whisk on high speed until the mixture is tripled in volume and the bowl is cool to the touch, about 10 minutes. Reduce the speed to low and whisk in the butter, about 4 tablespoons (2 oz/60 g) at a time, until incorporated. Continue to whisk until smooth and fluffy, about 10 minutes (the mixture may look grainy at first). Using a rubber spatula, fold in the smashed raspberries until no streaks remain.

7 Spoon the buttercream into a pastry bag fitted with a star tip (see page 123). Pipe the buttercream onto the cupcakes. Shave curls from the chunk of white chocolate (see page 122) and sprinkle over the cupcakes.

apricot-pistachio tart

MAKES 8 SERVINGS

1 sheet frozen all-butter puff
pastry, thawed according to
package directions

10 apricots, halved and pitted

2 tablespoons sugar

1 tablespoon orange liqueur

½ cup (5 oz/155 g) thick
apricot preserves

1 teaspoon ground cinnamon

½ teaspoon ground cardamom

6 tablespoons (1½ oz/45 g)
chopped pistachios

2 tablespoons honey

Apricots come into season in late spring or a little earlier in warm years. Their season is fleeting, so snap them up when you see them and make this easy-to-assemble tart. Look for all-butter puff pastry from a bakery or specialty-food shop, which will have the best flavor and texture.

1 Preheat the oven to 400°F (200°C). Have ready a 10-inch (25-cm) square tart pan with a removable bottom.

2 On a lightly floured surface, roll out the puff pastry sheet into an 11-inch (28-cm) square and transfer to the prepared pan (see page 117). Trim off the corners, then gather any dough overhang and press it into the sides of the pan to form a rim that is even in thickness. Using a fork, prick the bottom and sides of the dough. Place the tart shell in the freezer for 15 minutes. Remove from the freezer and bake until lightly golden, about 15 minutes. Let cool on a wire rack for about 30 minutes.

3 Meanwhile, in a bowl, stir together the apricots, sugar, and orange liqueur. Let the mixture stand at room temperature for 15 minutes.

4 Spread the apricot preserves evenly over the bottom of the tart shell. Sprinkle the cinnamon, cardamom, and 4 tablespoons (1 oz/30 g) of the

pistachios over the preserves. Arrange the apricots, cut sides down, on top and drizzle with any juices remaining in the bowl. Sprinkle the remaining 2 tablespoons pistachios over the top.

5 Bake until the apricots are tender and the pastry is golden brown, 30–40 minutes.

6 Remove the tart from the oven and drizzle the honey over the top. Let cool on a wire rack for about 1 hour. (The tart can be baked up to 4 hours in advance and cooled, then tented with aluminum foil and stored at room temperature.)

7 When ready to serve, set the pan sides fall away, then slide the tart onto a serving plate.

summer

peach lattice pie

MAKES 8 SERVINGS

3 lb (1.5 kg) peaches,
peeled (page 123)

5 tablespoons (2½ oz/75 g)
plus 2 teaspoons sugar

2 teaspoons fresh
lemon juice

3 tablespoons quick-
cooking tapioca

Double recipe Basic Pie Dough
(page 120), divided into
2 disks, one slightly
larger than the other

1 tablespoon all-purpose flour

1 large egg beaten with
1 tablespoon heavy cream

In some parts of the country, peach season can run for nearly four months, making this recipe indispensable to your pie repertoire. Be sure to choose ripe, juicy peaches that give slightly when gently squeezed. Better yet, ask for a sample at your local market to make sure the fruit has the perfect balance of tart and sweet.

1 Position a rack in the lower third of the oven and preheat to 400°F (200°C). Have ready a 9-inch (23-cm) pie pan.

2 Halve and pit the peaches, then cut them into slices about ½ inch (12 mm) thick. Place in a large bowl, add 4 tablespoons (2 oz/60 g) of the sugar, the lemon juice, and tapioca and stir gently to coat. Set aside.

3 On a lightly floured surface, roll out the larger dough disk into a 12-inch (30-cm) round about ⅛ inch (3 mm) thick. Transfer to the pie pan and fit the dough into the pan (see page 117). Sprinkle the flour and 1 tablespoon of the sugar over the crust. Pour the peach mixture into the crust and spread evenly. Roll out the smaller dough disk into a round about ⅛ inch (3 mm) thick. Using a pastry wheel, cut the dough into strips about ¾ inch (2 cm) wide.

4 To make the lattice, beginning about 1 inch (2.5 cm) from the edge of the pie pan, lay about 5 of the strips about 1 inch (2.5 cm) apart over

the filling. Fold back every other strip halfway over itself. Place a strip at a slight angle across the unfolded strips. Return the 2 strips that have been folded back to their flat position. Pull back the 3 alternate strips. Place the next strip across the unfolded strips about 1 inch (2.5 cm) from the last strip. Continue folding back and weaving strips until the top of the pie is latticed. Trim the dough overhang and then roll it under itself to make a rim. Gently brush the lattice with the egg mixture, then sprinkle with the 2 teaspoons sugar.

5 Bake until the edges of the crust begin to brown, about 15 minutes. Reduce the oven temperature to 350°F (180°C) and continue to bake until the crust is lightly browned and the filling is bubbling, 40–45 minutes, covering the edges with foil if the crust browns too quickly. Let cool completely on a wire rack, about 2 hours, before serving.

little plum galettes

MAKES 8 GALETTES

Double recipe Basic Pie Dough (page 120), divided into 2 disks

½ cup (4 oz/125 g) sugar, plus more for sprinkling

2 tablespoons cornstarch

¼ teaspoon ground cinnamon

⅛ teaspoon salt

2 lb (1 kg) plums, pitted and cut into small chunks (about 4 cups)

1 large egg beaten with 1 tablespoon heavy cream

Think of these charming desserts as individual rustic fruit pies. Pleating the edge of the crust over the filling gives the galettes a pretty appearance. When pleating the dough, work quickly so your fingers don't melt the butter in the dough, which will produce a tough crust.

1 Line 2 rimmed baking sheets with parchment paper.

2 On a lightly floured surface, roll out both dough disks into 12-inch (30-cm) rounds. Using a 6-inch (15-cm) cardboard circle and a small, sharp knife, cut out 3 or 4 rounds from each dough round. Press the scraps together and reroll to cut out more rounds. You should have a total of 8 rounds.

3 Place the dough rounds on the prepared baking sheets. Do not trim the edges of the dough.

4 In a small bowl, stir together the sugar, cornstarch, cinnamon, and salt. Place the plums in a large bowl, sprinkle with the sugar mixture, and toss to coat evenly.

5 Place about ½ cup (3 oz/90 g) of the plum mixture in the center of each dough round, leaving a 1-inch (2.5-cm) border all around. Fold the border up and over the filling of each tart, forming loose pleats all around the edges and leaving the centers open (see page 118). Refrigerate the galettes on the baking sheets until the dough is firm, 15–20 minutes.

6 Meanwhile, place a rack in the lower third of the oven and preheat to 375°F (190°C). Lightly brush the top crust with the egg mixture (you will not use all of it). Sprinkle the crust with sugar. Bake the galettes until the crusts are golden and the juice around the plums has thickened, about 40 minutes. Let cool on the baking sheets on a wire rack for about 15 minutes before serving.

dark cherry clafoutis

MAKES 6 SERVINGS

Unsalted butter
for greasing

1 lb (500 g) fresh dark
sweet cherries, pitted

1 cup (8 fl oz/250 ml)
whole milk

¼ cup (2 fl oz/60 ml)
heavy cream

½ cup (1½ oz/45 g)
sifted cake flour

4 large eggs, at room
temperature

½ cup (4 oz/125 g)
granulated sugar

⅛ teaspoon salt

½ teaspoon almond extract

Confectioners' sugar
for dusting

A country-style French dessert, a clafoutis consists of fresh fruit surrounded by a thick crepelike batter that is baked until golden brown. There's no need for a separate sauce; just lightly dust with confectioners' sugar for a pretty finishing touch.

1 Place a rack in the upper third of the oven and preheat to 350°F (180°C). Generously butter a shallow 1½-qt (1.5-l) baking dish.

2 Arrange the cherries in the prepared baking dish.

3 In a saucepan, combine the milk and cream. Place over medium-low heat and warm until small bubbles form around the edges. Remove from the heat and vigorously whisk in the flour, a little at a time, until no lumps remain.

4 In a bowl, whisk together the eggs, granulated sugar, and salt. Slowly whisk in the milk mixture and the almond extract to make a batter. Pour the batter over the cherries.

5 Place the dish on a baking sheet and bake until lightly browned, 45–55 minutes. Let cool on a wire rack for about 10 minutes. Dust with confectioners' sugar and serve warm.

blueberry–cream cheese custard pie

MAKES 8 SERVINGS

For the Crust

2 cups (7 oz/220 g) graham cracker pieces, crushed with a food processor or rolling pin

2 tablespoons sugar

Pinch of salt

½ cup (4 oz/125 g) unsalted butter, melted and cooled

For the Filling

½ lb (250 g) full-fat cream cheese, at room temperature

½ cup (4 oz/125 g) sugar

1 teaspoon vanilla extract

2 large eggs

½ lb (250 g) fresh blueberries (about 2 cups)

1½ tablespoons cornstarch mixed with 2 tablespoons water

This pie is a three-layer treat: a graham cracker crust; a baked cheesecake-like custard; and a thick, lightly simmered fresh blueberry topping. For best results, choose full-fat cream cheese over reduced-fat or nonfat varieties.

1 Preheat the oven to 325°F (165°C). Have ready a 9-inch (23-cm) pie pan.

2 To make the crust, in a bowl, stir together the graham cracker crumbs, sugar, and salt. Add the melted butter and stir until blended. Pat the crumb mixture evenly into the pan and up the sides. Bake until slightly firm, about 8 minutes. Let cool completely on a wire rack, about 30 minutes.

3 To make the filling, using an electric mixer, beat together the cream cheese, ¼ cup (3 oz/90 g) of the sugar, and the vanilla on medium speed until thoroughly blended and smooth, 3–5 minutes. Add the eggs 1 at a time and beat until well blended. Pour the filling into the crust and spread evenly.

4 Bake until the custard is just set, 25–30 minutes. Let cool on a wire rack for about 1 hour.

5 Meanwhile, in a saucepan, combine the blueberries, ½ cup (4 fl oz/ 125 ml) water, and the remaining ¼ cup (3 oz/90 g) sugar. Place over medium-high heat and bring to a boil. Reduce the heat to medium-low, cover, and simmer, stirring once, until the liquid is slightly reduced, about 5 minutes. Remove from the heat and add the cornstarch mixture. Return to medium-high heat, bring to a boil, and cook, stirring constantly, until thickened, about 1 minute. Remove from the heat and let cool until lukewarm, about 30 minutes.

6 Spoon the berries over the custard. Refrigerate the pie for at least 1 hour and up to 24 hours before serving.

nectarine streusel coffee cake

Unsalted butter for greasing

All-purpose flour for dusting

For the Streusel

¾ cup (4 oz/125 g) all-purpose flour

⅓ cup (2½ oz/75 g) firmly packed light brown sugar

¼ cup (2 oz/60 g) granulated sugar

1 teaspoon ground cinnamon

6 tablespoons (3 oz/90 g) cold unsalted butter, cut into pieces

For the Cake

1½ cups (7½ oz/235 g) all-purpose flour

¾ cup (6 oz/185 g) granulated sugar

2 teaspoons baking powder

½ teaspoon salt

1 large egg, at room temperature

4 tablespoons (2 oz/60 g) unsalted butter, melted and cooled

½ cup (4 fl oz/125 ml) whole milk, at room temperature

1½ teaspoons vanilla extract

1 teaspoon almond extract

1 lb (500 g) firm, ripe nectarines, pitted and sliced

This streusel-topped coffee cake works with any type of stone fruit—peaches, plums, and pluots—but we especially like the way the buttery, cinnamon-scented flavors work with nectarines. If you choose peaches and they are very fuzzy, you may want to peel them first (page 123).

1 Preheat the oven to 350°F (180°C). Butter and flour a 9-inch (23-cm) square baking pan and tap out the excess flour.

2 To make the streusel, in a bowl, stir together the flour, brown sugar, granulated sugar, and cinnamon. Using a pastry blender or your fingers, cut or rub in the butter until coarse crumbs form. Set aside.

3 To make the cake, in a bowl, whisk together the flour, granulated sugar, baking powder, and salt; set aside.

4 In another bowl, using an electric mixer on medium speed, beat together the egg, melted butter, milk, vanilla, and almond extract until creamy, about 1 minute. Add to the flour mixture to the egg mixture and beat just until evenly moistened. There should be no lumps or dry spots. Do not overmix.

5 Pour the batter into the prepared pan and spread evenly. Arrange the nectarine slices in rows on top of the batter. Gently press the slices into the batter and sprinkle with the streusel.

6 Bake until the topping is golden brown and a tester inserted into the center of the cake comes out clean, 40–45 minutes. Let cool on a wire rack for 20 minutes. Serve warm or at room temperature, cut into squares.

blackberry turnovers

MAKES 8 TURNOVERS

½ lb (250 g) fresh
blackberries (about 2 cups)

½ cup (4 oz/125 g)
granulated sugar

¼ cup (1 oz/30 g) cornstarch

Large pinch of salt

2 sheets frozen all-butter puff
pastry, thawed according to
package directions

1 large egg beaten with
1 tablespoon heavy cream

Turbinado sugar for sprinkling

What could be better than blackberry pie? Not much, except maybe these individual handheld pies. They call for just five ingredients, and using frozen puff pastry means you can make them anytime a sweet craving strikes.

1 Line a rimmed baking sheet with parchment paper.

2 In a saucepan, combine the blackberries, granulated sugar, cornstarch, salt, and 2 tablespoons water. Place over low heat and cook, stirring constantly, until the mixture is thick and jamlike, about 5 minutes. Transfer to a bowl and cover with plastic wrap, pressing it directly onto the surface of the berries. Refrigerate until completely cool, about 1 hour.

3 On a lightly floured surface, roll out and/or cut 1 puff pastry sheet to make a 10-inch (25-cm) square. Trim $\frac{1}{16}$ inch (2 mm) off the edges and cut the pastry into 4 equal squares. Spoon about 2 tablespoons of the berry mixture into the center of each square. Lightly brush the edges of each square with water and fold in half to form a triangle. Gently press the edges together with the tines of a fork to seal. Place the turnovers on the prepared baking sheet about 2 inches (5 cm) apart. Repeat with the remaining puff pastry and berry mixture. Refrigerate for 15 minutes. Meanwhile, preheat the oven to 375°F (190°C).

4 Brush the tops of the turnovers lightly with the egg mixture, then sprinkle with turbinado sugar. Bake until puffed and golden brown, 25–35 minutes. Let cool on the pan on a wire rack for 20 minutes, then serve warm.

plum frangipane tart

MAKES 8 SERVINGS

Basic Tart Dough (page 120)

1 cup (5½ oz/170 g) blanched almonds

⅔ cup (5 oz/155 g) plus 1 tablespoon sugar

¼ teaspoon salt

1 teaspoon vanilla extract

½ teaspoon almond extract

1 large egg

4 tablespoons (2 oz/60 g) unsalted butter, at room temperature

8 plums, pitted and quartered

Frangipane is a mixture of ground almonds, sugar, eggs, and butter, which bakes into a soft, macaronlike layer in this summertime tart. The dessert takes only minutes to prepare, especially if you make the dough in advance.

1 On a lightly floured surface, roll out the dough into a 12-inch (30-cm) round about ⅛ inch (3 mm) thick. Transfer to a 9½-inch (24-cm) tart pan with a removable bottom, and fit the dough into the pan (see page 117). Trim off any excess by gently running a rolling pin across the top of the pan. Press the dough into the sides of the pan so that it extends slightly above the rim. Refrigerate or freeze the tart shell until firm, about 30 minutes.

2 Meanwhile, place a rack in the lower third of the oven and preheat to 375°F (190°C). Partially bake the tart shell (see page 122). Set the tart shell on a wire rack to cool slightly. Reduce the oven heat to 350°F (180°C).

3 In a food processor, combine the almonds and the ⅔ cup (5 oz/155 g) sugar and process until the almonds are finely ground. Add the salt, vanilla

and almond extracts, and egg and process until blended. Add the butter and process until the mixture is smooth. Using a rubber spatula, scrape the almond mixture into the tart shell and spread evenly. Arrange the plum quarters, cut side up, on top in 2 concentric circles. Sprinkle the remaining 1 tablespoon sugar over the plums.

4 Bake until the filling is golden and set when you give the pan a gentle shake, 30–35 minutes. Let cool completely on a wire rack, about 1 hour.

5 To serve, let the sides fall away from the pan, then slide the tart onto a serving plate. Serve at room temperature.

black forest cake with fresh cherries

MAKES 10–12 SERVINGS

Unsalted butter for greasing

1 cup (5 oz/155 g) all-purpose flour, plus flour for dusting

⅔ cup (2 oz/60 g) Dutch-process cocoa powder

¼ teaspoon salt

9 large eggs, separated, at room temperature

1¾ cups (14 oz/435 g) sugar

1 teaspoon vanilla extract

¾ teaspoon almond extract

½ teaspoon cream of tartar

Fresh Cherry Filling and Syrup (page 122)

Kirsch Whipped Cream (page 121)

6-oz (185-g) block semisweet chocolate, shaved (see page 122)

Fresh cherries, dark chocolate, and whipped cream combine in this classic Viennese cake. The cherry flavor is enhanced by a good measure of kirsch, which is stirred into both the filling and the whipped cream frosting.

1 Preheat the oven to 325°F (165°C). Butter two 9-inch (23-cm) round cake pans and line with parchment paper. Butter and flour the paper.

2 Sift together the flour, cocoa powder, and salt onto a sheet of parchment; set aside. Using a stand mixer with the paddle attachment, beat together the egg yolks and 1 cup (8 oz/250 g) of the sugar on medium speed until light and fluffy, about 3 minutes. Beat in the extracts.

3 Using a clean bowl and clean whisk attachment, whisk together the egg whites and cream of tartar on medium speed until the whites thicken. Increase the speed to medium-high and beat just until soft peaks form, about 3 minutes. Slowly add the remaining ¾ cup (6 oz/185 g) sugar and continue to beat until stiff, glossy peaks form, about 2 more minutes. Using a rubber spatula, gently fold one-third of the egg whites into the egg yolk mixture until almost incorporated. Fold in half of the flour mixture. Fold in another one-third of the whites, followed by the remaining flour. Fold in the remaining whites until

the batter is smooth and no whites are visible. Divide the batter among the prepared pans

4 Bake until a tester inserted into the center of the cakes comes out clean, about 35 minutes. Immediately run a small, thin knife around the inside of each pan to loosen the cakes. Let cool in the pans on a wire rack for 10 minutes. Invert the cakes onto wire racks, peel off the parchment, and turn upright. Let cool completely, about 1 hour.

5 To assemble, cut each cake layer in half horizontally. Place 1 cake layer on a platter and generously brush with cherry syrup. Using a spatula, spread about one-fourth of the Kirsch Whipped Cream over the cake. Arrange one-third of the reserved cherry pieces in an even layer over the cream. Repeat the process with 2 more cake layers, using all of the cherries. Place the remaining layer on top and brush the top and sides with the syrup. Spread with the remaining whipped cream over the top. Top with chocolate shavings and serve.

blackberry slab pie

MAKES 20 SERVINGS

Triple recipe Basic
Pie Dough (page 120),
divided into 2 disks

1 cup (8 oz/250 g) sugar

¼ cup (1 oz/30 g) quick-
cooking tapioca

½ teaspoon ground cinnamon

¼ teaspoon allspice

¼ teaspoon salt

2 teaspoons grated lemon zest

2 lb (1 kg) fresh blackberries
(about 6 cups)

3 tablespoons unsalted butter,
cut into small pieces

Slab pie really is a genius dessert. It has all the elements
of the traditional round version—a flaky crust bursting
with fresh fruit. But unlike a regular pie, a slab pie will
feed a crowd, is easier to make, and is less fussy to serve.
You can use any type of berry—raspberry, marionberry,
olallieberry—but blackberries are always a favorite.

1 Place a rack in the lower third of the oven and preheat to 375°F (190°C).

2 On a lightly floured surface, roll out 1 dough disk into an 18-by-14-inch (45-by-35-cm) rectangle. Transfer to a jelly-roll pan and fit the dough into the bottom and up the sides of the pan. Roll out the other dough disk on a piece of parchment paper into the same-size rectangle.

3 In a large bowl, gently stir together the sugar, tapioca, cinnamon, allspice, salt, lemon zest, and blackberries. Pour the filling into the crust in the pan and spread evenly. Dot with the butter. Using the parchment to help you, invert the rolled-out crust over the filling, lining up the edges. Peel off the parchment.

Trim the dough edges, leaving a ¾-inch (2-cm) overhang. Fold the overhang under itself and crimp decoratively (see page 118) Cut a few steam vents in the top crust.

4 Bake until the crust is golden brown and the filling is bubbling, 45–50 minutes, tenting the pie edges with aluminum foil if the crust browns too quickly.

5 Let cool completely on a wire rack before serving, at least 2 hours. (Note: The pie can be prepared through step 3, covered securely with aluminum foil, and frozen for up to 2 weeks. Bake the frozen pie for an additional 10–15 minutes.)

blueberry crumble pie

MAKES 8 SERVINGS

Basic Pie Dough (page 120)

For the Topping

¾ cup (4 oz/125 g)
all-purpose flour

⅓ cup (2½ oz/45 g) firmly
packed light brown sugar

⅓ cup (3 oz/90 g)
granulated sugar

1 teaspoon ground cinnamon

⅛ teaspoon salt

½ cup (4 oz/125 g) cold
unsalted butter, cut into
¾-inch (2-cm) pieces

For the Filling

1¼ lb (625 g) fresh
blueberries (about 5 cups)

Finely grated zest of 1 lemon

⅓ cup (2½ oz/45 g) firmly
packed light brown sugar

1 teaspoon ground cinnamon

5 tablespoons (2 oz/60 g)
all-purpose flour

1 tablespoon granulated sugar

A crunchy crumb topping perfectly accents the juicy blueberries in this tempting summer pie. Ground cinnamon and grated lemon zest bring out the natural flavor of the berries. The pie is best served the day it is baked, so it's a great addition to a cookout in the heat of summer.

1 Preheat the oven to 400°F (200°C). Have ready a 9-inch (23-cm) pie pan.

2 On a lightly floured surface, roll out the dough into a 12-inch (30-cm) round about ⅛ inch (3 mm) thick. Transfer to the pie pan and fit the dough into the pan (see page 117). Trim the edges, leaving a ¾-inch (2-cm) overhang. Fold the overhang under itself and crimp decoratively (see page 118). Bake the crust partially (see page 122). Let the pie shell cool completely on a wire rack, about 30 minutes. Reduce the oven temperature to 375°F (190°C).

3 To make the topping, in a large bowl, stir together the ¾ cup (4 oz/125 g) flour, ⅓ cup (2½ oz/75 g) of the brown sugar, the ⅓ cup (3 oz/90 g) granulated sugar, 1 teaspoon of the cinnamon, and the salt. Scatter the butter pieces on top and toss with a fork or your fingers to coat with the flour mixture. Using your fingertips or a pastry blender, work the

ingredients together until the mixture forms large, coarse crumbs the size of large peas. Set the topping aside.

4 In a large bowl, gently stir together the blueberries, lemon zest, the remaining ⅓ cup (2½ oz/75 g) brown sugar, the remaining 1 teaspoon cinnamon, and 4 tablespoons (1½ oz/45 g) of the flour to coat the berries evenly. Sprinkle the remaining 1 tablespoon flour and granulated sugar over the bottom of the crust. Pour the filling into the crust and spread evenly. Sprinkle the topping over the filling.

5 Bake until the topping is golden brown and the filling just begins to bubble, 50–60 minutes, covering the edges with aluminum foil if the crust browns too quickly. Let cool completely on a wire rack, about 2 hours, before serving.

honey-roasted stone fruit with thyme

MAKES 4–6 SERVINGS

2 tablespoons unsalted butter, cut into 12 pieces, plus melted butter for greasing

¼ cup (2 oz/60 g) firmly packed light brown sugar

2-inch (5-cm) piece vanilla bean, split lengthwise

6 large ripe stone fruits, such as peaches, plums, nectarines, or pluots, halved and pitted

4 tablespoons (3 oz/90 g) honey

3 fresh thyme sprigs

Vanilla Whipped Cream (page 120) for serving

One of the best things about stone fruits is that they are nearly interchangeable in baking recipes, so you can choose what looks and tastes best at the market, or whatever fruit your family prefers. Roasting stone fruits intensifies their natural flavors, and the vanilla bean and fresh thyme in this recipe lend exotic accents.

1 Preheat the oven to 400°F (200°C). Line a large baking pan with aluminum foil and brush the foil with melted butter.

2 Put the brown sugar in a small bowl. Using the tip of a small knife, scrape the seeds from the vanilla bean into the bowl and stir to mix well. Place the stone fruits, cut side up, in a single layer in the prepared pan. Drizzle 2 tablespoons of the honey evenly over the fruit and sprinkle with the brown sugar mixture.

Dot the fruit with the butter and strew the thyme sprigs over the top.

3 Roast until the fruit is tender and browned, about 20 minutes. Divide the fruit among serving dishes. Drizzle with any syrup remaining in the pan and then with the remaining 2 tablespoons honey. Top with dollops of vanilla whipped cream and serve right away.

plum buckle

Vegetable oil spray

**1½ cups (7½ oz/235 g)
all-purpose flour**

1 teaspoon baking powder

¼ teaspoon salt

**1 cup (8 oz/250 g) unsalted
butter, at room temperature**

**1 cup (8 oz/250 g) plus
1 tablespoon sugar**

**2 large eggs, at room
temperature**

**1 lb (500 g) plums, halved,
pitted, and each half
cut into 4 slices**

¼ teaspoon ground cinnamon

A buckle is essentially cake on the bottom with fresh fruit on the top. As it bakes, the weight of the fruit causes the cake to sink slightly, lending a homey appearance. Fresh plums are available throughout the summer in a variety of colors, from yellow and green to deep pink, purple, and scarlet. Choose fragrant plums with sweet, tangy flesh.

1 Place a rack in the lower third of the oven and preheat to 350°F (180°C). Coat an 8-inch (20-cm) square cake pan with vegetable oil spray. Line the bottom with parchment paper and coat with more spray.

2 In a bowl, whisk together the flour, baking powder, and salt; set aside.

3 Using an electric mixer, beat together the butter and the 1 cup (8 oz/250 g) sugar on medium speed until pale and fluffy, 3–5 minutes. Add the eggs 1 at a time, beating well after each addition. Add the flour mixture, reduce the mixer speed to low, and beat until well blended.

4 Pour the batter into the prepared pan and spread evenly. Poke the plum slices into the batter, placing them close together. In a small bowl, stir together the cinnamon and the 1 tablespoon sugar. Sprinkle over the batter.

5 Bake until the top is golden, the edges pull away from the pan, and a tester inserted into the center of the buckle comes out clean, 50–60 minutes. Let cool on a wire rack for about 30 minutes before serving.

individual bing cherry cobblers

MAKES 6 COBBLERS

For the Filling

3 lb (1.5 kg) fresh Bing cherries or other sweet cherries, pitted

1 tablespoon fresh lemon juice

3 tablespoons sugar

For the Topping

⅔ cup (5 fl oz/160 ml) buttermilk

1 teaspoon vanilla extract

1½ cups (7½ oz/235 g) all-purpose flour

⅓ cup (3 oz/90 g) plus 1 tablespoon sugar

1 teaspoon baking powder

½ teaspoon baking soda

½ teaspoon salt

¾ teaspoon ground cinnamon

6 tablespoons (3 oz/90 g) cold unsalted butter, cut into ½-inch (12-mm) pieces

A cobbler consists of a biscuitlike topping and a fresh fruit filling. As the cobbler bakes, the topping forms a golden brown crust atop the bubbling fruit below. This recipe uses a soft biscuit dough that spreads as it bakes to cover the fruit completely, like an upside-down pie. Serve with cold heavy cream poured over the top, if desired.

1 Preheat the oven to 375°F (190°C). Place six 1-cup (8–fl oz/250-ml) ramekins or custard cups on a rimmed baking sheet.

2 To make the filling, in a large bowl, stir together the cherries, lemon juice, and the 3 tablespoons sugar until well mixed. Divide the fruit mixture among the ramekins. Bake for 10 minutes.

3 To make the topping, in a small bowl, stir together the buttermilk and vanilla; set aside. In a large bowl, sift together the flour, sugar, baking powder, baking soda, salt, and ½ teaspoon of the cinnamon. Using a pastry blender or 2 knives, cut in the butter until the mixture forms large, coarse crumbs the size of small peas. Pour the buttermilk mixture over the flour mixture and, using a large wooden spoon, stir just until combined and a soft, sticky, evenly moistened dough forms.

4 Drop the dough by heaping spoonfuls onto the hot fruit, spacing it evenly over the surface. The topping will not cover the fruit but will spread during baking. In a small bowl, stir together the remaining 1 tablespoon sugar and ¼ teaspoon cinnamon. Sprinkle over the dough.

5 Bake until the fruit filling is bubbling, the topping is browned, and a tester inserted into the topping comes out clean, 30–35 minutes. Let cool on a wire rack for 15 minutes. Serve warm.

warm peach cake

MAKES 8 SERVINGS

For the Cake

½ cup (4 oz/125 g) unsalted
butter, melted and cooled,
plus butter for greasing

1½ cups (7½ oz/235 g)
all-purpose flour, plus
flour for dusting

2 lb (1 kg) peaches, peeled
(page 123)

2 tablespoons fresh
lemon juice

½ cup (4 oz/125 g)
granulated sugar

2 teaspoons baking powder

½ teaspoon salt

2 large eggs, at room
temperature

3 tablespoons whole milk,
at room temperature

Grated zest of 1 lemon

For the Topping

½ cup (3½ oz/105 g) firmly
packed dark brown sugar

½ teaspoon ground cinnamon

½ teaspoon ground ginger

Vanilla Whipped Cream
(page 120) for serving

This is one of the first recipes we make when our favorite peaches arrive in the farmers' market. It features a lemon-scented batter topped with a layer of fresh fruit and a simple topping made with brown sugar and spices. Serve slices with a cup of hot tea or coffee.

1 Preheat the oven to 375°F (190°C). Butter and flour a 9-inch (23-cm) springform pan and tap out the excess flour.

2 To make the cake, halve and pit the peaches, then cut them into slices about ¾ inch (2 cm) thick. Place in a large bowl, add the lemon juice, and stir gently to coat. Set aside.

3 In a bowl, sift together the flour, granulated sugar, baking powder, and salt. In another bowl, beat together the eggs and milk, then beat in the melted butter and lemon zest. Slowly pour the egg mixture into the flour mixture, stirring with a fork just to moisten the dry ingredients. Do not overmix. Pour the batter into the prepared pan and spread evenly. Drain the peaches, reserving the liquid, and arrange the slices in a spiral design on top of the batter. Drizzle the liquid over the peaches.

4 To make the topping, in a bowl, using a fork, stir together the brown sugar, cinnamon, and ginger. Sprinkle over the peaches.

5 Bake until a tester inserted into the center of the cake comes out clean, about 35 minutes. Let cool on a wire rack for 15 minutes. Release the pan sides and place the cake on a plate. Serve warm, topped with whipped cream.

sour cherry pie

MAKES 8 SERVINGS

**Double recipe Basic
Pie Dough (page 120),
divided into 2 disks**

½ cup (4 oz/125 g) sugar

**¼ cup (1½ oz/45 g)
all-purpose flour**

**2 lb (1 kg) fresh sour
cherries, pitted**

**1 tablespoon unsalted butter,
cut into small pieces**

Every summer we look forward to sour cherry season.
The fruits are usually only in the markets for a week or two,
so we buy them in large quantities to make this classic
double-crust pie. The filling uses just four ingredients,
so the true flavor of the fruit really shines through.

1 Preheat the oven to 425°F (220°C).
Have ready a 9-inch (23-cm) pie pan.

2 On a lightly floured surface, roll
out 1 dough disk into a 12-inch
(30-cm) round about ⅛ inch (3 mm)
thick. Transfer to the pie pan and fit
the dough into the pan (see page 117).
Roll out the other dough disk for the
top crust into the same-size round.

3 In a bowl, stir together the sugar
and flour. Add the cherries and stir
to coat. Pour the filling into the crust and
spread evenly. Dot with the butter. Place
the top crust over the filling and trim the
edges, leaving a ¾-inch (2-cm) overhang.
Fold the overhang under itself and crimp
decoratively (see page 118). Cut a few
steam vents in the top crust.

4 Place the pie on a baking sheet
and bake for 15 minutes. Reduce
the oven temperature to 350°F (180°C)
and continue to bake until the cherries
are soft when pierced through one
of the slits, 20–25 minutes, covering the
edges with aluminum foil if the crust
browns too quickly. Let cool on a wire
rack for at least 2 hours before serving.

fall

roasted grape tartlets

MAKES 6 TARTLETS

1½ lb (750 g) seedless
red grapes

1½ teaspoons olive oil

Kosher salt

3 tablespoons plus
2 teaspoons sugar

1 sheet frozen all-butter puff
pastry, thawed according to
package directions

1 cup (9 oz/280 g)
mascarpone cheese

Finely grated zest of ½ lemon

½ teaspoon vanilla extract

Whole milk or heavy cream,
if needed

These pretty little tartlets are best made in early autumn during grape harvest. Creamy mascarpone cheese is highlighted with vanilla and lemon zest, then smeared over buttery puff pastry and topped off with sugared roasted grapes. Roasting the grapes gives them a lovely mellow flavor. This recipe is easily doubled for a gathering.

1 Preheat the oven to 450°F (230°C). Have ready 2 rimmed baking sheets.

2 Spread the grapes on 1 baking sheet, drizzle with the olive oil, and sprinkle with a little salt. Roast, stirring once or twice, until the grapes begin to burst, about 10 minutes. Toss the hot grapes with the 2 teaspoons sugar. Let cool.

3 Reduce the oven temperature to 400°F (200°C). Line the other baking sheet with parchment paper.

4 On a lightly floured surface, roll out the puff pastry into a 12-by-14-inch (30-by-35-cm) rectangle. Trim the edges evenly and cut the large rectangle into 6 equal rectangles. Using a fork, prick the pastry all over. Place the rectangles on the prepared baking sheet and freeze for 15 minutes.

5 Meanwhile, in a bowl, stir together the mascarpone, lemon zest, the 3 tablespoons sugar, the vanilla, and ¼ teaspoon salt; the mixture should be spreadable (if not, stir in a small amount of milk or cream). Dollop about 2 tablespoons of the mascarpone mixture into the center of each pastry rectangle, spreading it almost to the edges.

6 Bake the pastry rectangles until the pastry is crisp and golden, 15–20 minutes. Transfer the pastry to a wire rack and cool for 10 minutes.

7 Place the pastry rectangles on plates and top with the roasted grapes, dividing evenly. Serve right away.

spiced pear tarte tatin

MAKES 8 SERVINGS

3 tablespoons unsalted butter

**¼ cup (2 oz/60 g)
granulated sugar**

**4 firm, ripe, Bosc or Anjou
pears, peeled, cored,
and quartered**

**½ cup (4 oz/120 g) firmly
packed light brown sugar**

**2 tablespoons finely chopped
crystallized ginger**

1 tablespoon fresh lemon juice

½ teaspoon ground cinnamon

¼ teaspoon ground nutmeg

¼ teaspoon ground cloves

**1 sheet frozen all-butter puff
pastry, thawed according
to package directions**

This French-style upside-down tart is classically made with apples, but we also like our spiced pear variation. The dramatic presentation—caramelized pear wedges nestled in a disk of golden brown pastry—belies how easy it is to put together. Starting with a good-quality, purchased puff pastry dough keeps prep to a minimum.

1 Preheat the oven to 375°F (190°C). Using 1 tablespoon of the butter, grease a 12-inch (30-cm) round baking dish with 2-inch (5-cm) sides. Sprinkle the granulated sugar evenly over the bottom.

2 Place the pears, cut side up, in a tight layer in the prepared baking dish. Sprinkle with ¼ cup (2 oz/60 g) of the brown sugar, the crystallized ginger, and the lemon juice. Cut the remaining 2 tablespoons butter into bits and dot the tops of the pears. In a small bowl, stir together the remaining ¼ cup (2 oz/60 g) brown sugar, the cinnamon, nutmeg, and cloves. Sprinkle the mixture over the pears.

3 On a lightly floured surface, roll out the puff pastry a little larger than the diameter of the baking dish. Cover the dish with the pastry, tucking the edges into the dish to form a rim that encircles the pears. Prick the pastry all over with a fork.

4 Bake until the pastry is golden brown, the pears are tender, and a thickened, golden syrup has formed in the dish, about 1 hour. Let cool on a wire rack for 5 minutes.

5 Run a knife around the inside of the dish to loosen the tart. Invert the tart onto a plate, dislodging and replacing any pears that may have stuck to the dish. Cut into wedges and serve warm.

quince tea cake

MAKES 8 SERVINGS

¾ cup (6 oz/185 g) firmly packed light brown sugar

1 cinnamon stick, lightly crushed

Grated zest of 1 orange

1 tablespoon fresh orange juice

2 quinces, peeled, cored, and each cut into 8 wedges

¾ cup (6 oz/185 g) unsalted butter, at room temperature, plus butter for greasing

1½ cups (7½ oz/235 g) all-purpose flour, plus flour for dusting

1½ teaspoons baking powder

Pinch of salt

¾ cup (6 oz/185 g) granulated sugar

1 teaspoon vanilla extract

3 large eggs, at room temperature

For this simple yet elegant cake, quince wedges are first poached in a spiced syrup, then they're diced and mixed into a butter-rich cake batter. The poaching syrup becomes a sweet sauce that is drizzled over the top of the cake slices after baking.

1 In a saucepan, combine the brown sugar, cinnamon stick, orange zest, orange juice, and 2½ cups (20 fl oz/625 ml) water. Place over medium-high heat and cook, stirring, until the sugar dissolves. Add the quinces and bring to a boil. Reduce the heat to medium-low and simmer until tender when pierced with the tip of a paring knife, 45–60 minutes. Let the quinces cool in the syrup, then transfer to a cutting board and cut into ½-inch (12-mm) dice. Strain the syrup and set aside.

2 Preheat the oven to 325°F (165°C). Butter and flour a 9-inch (23-cm) round cake pan. Tap out the excess flour.

3 In a bowl, whisk together the flour, baking powder, and salt; set aside.

4 Using an electric mixer, beat together the butter and granulated sugar on medium speed until light and fluffy, 3–5 minutes. Beat in the vanilla. Add the eggs 1 at a time, beating well after each addition. Using a rubber spatula, fold in the flour mixture and diced quince. Pour the batter into the prepared pan and spread evenly.

5 Bake until a tester inserted into the center of the cake comes out clean, 35–40 minutes. Let cool on a wire rack for 10 minutes, then remove the cake from the pan and let cool completely on the rack, about 1 hour. Cut the cake into slices, drizzle with the reserved syrup, and serve.

frosted apple cake

MAKES 12 SERVINGS

2 cups (10 oz/315 g)
all-purpose flour

1 teaspoon baking powder

1 teaspoon baking soda

1 teaspoon ground cinnamon

½ teaspoon ground nutmeg

½ teaspoon ground cloves

½ teaspoon salt

¾ cup (6 oz/185 g) unsalted
butter, at room temperature

1½ cups (12 oz/375 g) sugar

3 large eggs, at room
temperature

½ cup (4 fl oz/125 ml)
buttermilk, at room
temperature

2 cups (8 oz/250 g) diced,
peeled apples (about
2½ apples)

½ cup (2 oz/60 g) walnuts,
toasted (page 123) and
chopped (optional)

Cream Cheese Frosting
(page 121)

Think of this cake when you need a sweet treat to serve a crowd. It's great for an after-school snack or play dates at your house, as well as for a casual get-together with friends. Use a soft, tart apple, such as Gravenstein or McIntosh. Pippin or Granny Smith apples work well, too.

1 Preheat the oven to 350°F (180°C). Line a 9-by-13-inch (23-by-33-cm) baking pan with parchment paper, letting the paper hang over the sides by several inches.

2 To make the cake, sift together the flour, baking powder, baking soda, cinnamon, nutmeg, cloves, and salt onto a sheet of parchment paper; set aside.

3 Using an electric mixer, beat together the butter and sugar on medium-high speed until light and fluffy, 3–5 minutes. Add the eggs 1 at a time, beating well after each addition.

4 Using a rubber spatula, gently fold in the flour mixture in 3 additions alternately with the buttermilk in 2 additions, starting and ending with the flour mixture. Then fold in the apples and walnuts, if using. Using a light lifting motion and turning the bowl continuously, fold in until the batter is smooth and the flour is thoroughly incorporated. Do not fold too vigorously or the cake will be tough. Pour the batter into the prepared pan and spread evenly.

5 Bake until the top is brown and a tester inserted into the center of the cake comes out clean, 35–40 minutes. Let cool on a wire rack.

6 When the cake is cool, grasp the edges of the parchment paper and lift up to remove the cake from the pan. Place the cake on a work surface. Using a long cake spatula, spread the frosting over the surface of the cake. Cut the cake into squares and serve.

baked stuffed apples

MAKES 4 SERVINGS

4 firm, sweet-tart apples

¼ cup (1½ oz/45 g)
dried currants

¼ cup (1 oz/30 g)
chopped walnuts

4 cinnamon sticks

4 tablespoons (2 oz/60 g)
firmly packed light
brown sugar

¼ cup (3 fl oz/85 ml)
pure maple syrup

Crème Anglaise (page 121) or
vanilla ice cream for serving

Here, apples are stuffed with dried fruit, nuts, and cinnamon sticks for a comforting dessert on a cold fall evening. The best apples for baking have a full, slightly tart flavor and hold their shape in the intense heat of the oven. Braeburn, Jonathan, and Winesap are all good choices. Visit your local farmers' markets to find regional varieties.

1 Preheat the oven to 350°F (180°C). Select a baking sheet that will hold the apples with about 1 inch (2.5 cm) of space between each one.

2 Using an apple corer, core the apples and then peel the skin from the top one-third of each apple. If necessary, cut a thin slice off the blossom (bottom) end so that the apples will stand upright. Place in the baking dish.

3 In a small bowl, stir together the currants and walnuts. Insert a cinnamon stick in the hollow center of each apple, then stuff each one with the currant-walnut mixture, dividing evenly.

Pat 1 tablespoon brown sugar on top of each apple. Drizzle the maple syrup evenly over the apples.

4 Cover the baking dish tightly with aluminum foil. Bake the apples, basting them occasionally with their juices, until they are tender when pierced with a skewer or small knife, 1–1½ hours. The timing will depend on the size of the apples.

5 Let the apples cool for about 5 minutes. Serve the apples warm with a drizzle of their juices and a spoonful of Crème Anglaise or a scoop of vanilla ice cream.

fresh fig galette

MAKES 8 SERVINGS

Basic Pie Dough (page 120)

16 fresh figs, stemmed and quartered lengthwise

¼ cup (2 oz/60 g) firmly packed light brown sugar

2 tablespoons all-purpose flour

1 tablespoon fresh lemon juice

½ teaspoon almond extract

2 tablespoons granulated sugar

1 large egg beaten with 1 tablespoon heavy cream

Figs should be harvested when fully ripened, so look for plump, soft fruits that do not give off a milky substance when the stem is broken. Use them as soon as possible, storing them unwashed for no more than a day in the refrigerator. The galette is best served the day it is baked.

1 Place a rack in the lower third of the oven and preheat to 400°F (200°C). Line a rimmed baking sheet with parchment paper.

2 On a lightly floured surface, roll out the dough into a 12-inch (30-cm) round about ⅛ inch (3 mm) thick. Transfer to the prepared baking sheet.

3 In a large bowl, combine the figs, brown sugar, 1 tablespoon of the flour, the lemon juice, and almond extract and gently stir together. Sprinkle the remaining 1 tablespoon flour and 1 tablespoon of the granulated sugar over the pastry, leaving a 2-inch (5-cm) border uncovered. Arrange the fig mixture in the center of the dough, keeping it off the border. Fold the border up and over the filling, forming loose pleats all around the edge and leaving the center open (see page 118). Brush the pleated dough with the egg mixture (you will not use all of it), then sprinkle the top of the dough with the remaining 1 tablespoon granulated sugar.

4 Bake until the crust is golden brown and the figs are soft, 30–40 minutes. Let the galette cool on the baking sheet on a wire rack for at least 15 minutes. Serve warm or at room temperature.

double-crust apple pie

2½ lb (1.25 kg) apples, peeled, cored, and cut into ¼-inch (6-mm) slices

1 tablespoon fresh lemon juice

2 tablespoons unsalted butter, melted and cooled

¼ cup (2 oz/60 g) firmly packed light brown sugar

1¾ teaspoons ground cinnamon

⅛ teaspoon ground nutmeg

Double recipe Basic Pie Dough (page 120), divided into 2 disks

1 large egg beaten with 2 tablespoons heavy cream

1 tablespoon granulated sugar

This iconic holiday pie is the perfect one for a Thanksgiving table. Try Granny Smith, Rome Beauty, or Baldwin apples, which all boast a bit of tartness along with their sweet qualities and hold their shape well during baking. We like to adorn the top crust with leaf-shaped cutouts, attached with an egg wash (see page 122), to evoke the fall theme.

1 Place a rack in the lower third of the oven and preheat to 400°F (200°C). Have ready a 9-inch (23-cm) pie dish or pan.

2 In a large bowl, stir together the apples, lemon juice, melted butter, brown sugar, 1½ teaspoons of the cinnamon, and the nutmeg.

3 On a lightly floured surface, roll out 1 dough disk into a 12-inch (30-cm) round about ⅛ inch (3 mm) thick. Transfer to the pan and fit the dough into the pan (see page 117). Roll out the other dough disk for the top crust into the same-sized round.

4 Stir the filling again, pour it into the crust, and spread evenly. Place the top crust over the filling and trim the edges, leaving a ¾-inch (2-cm) overhang. Fold the overhang under itself and crimp decoratively (see page 118). Brush the top of the pie, but not the crimped edges, with the egg mixture (you will not use all of it). In a small bowl, stir together the granulated sugar and the remaining ¼ teaspoon cinnamon. Sprinkle over the pie. Cut a few steam vents in the top crust.

5 Bake for 15 minutes. Reduce the oven temperature to 350°F (180°C) and continue to bake until the crust is lightly browned, the filling is bubbling, and the apples are tender when pierced through one of the slits, 40–45 minutes, covering the edges with aluminum foil if the crust browns too quickly. Let cool on a wire rack for about 20 minutes and serve warm, or let cool completely, about 2 hours, and serve at room temperature.

pumpkin-ginger cheesecake

MAKES 12 SERVINGS

For the Crust

2½ cups (6 oz/185 g) finely ground gingersnap cookies

¾ cup (5 oz/155 g) finely ground walnuts

¼ cup (2 oz/60 g) granulated sugar

5 tablespoons (2½ oz/75 g) unsalted butter, melted and cooled

For the Filling

1 lb (500 g) full-fat cream cheese, at room temperature

¾ cup (6 oz/185 g) firmly packed light brown sugar

2 large eggs

3⅓ cups (26½ oz/830 g) Roasted Pumpkin Purée (page 122)

½ cup (4 fl oz/125 ml) heavy cream

1 teaspoon ground cinnamon

½ teaspoon ground ginger

½ teaspoon ground nutmeg

A fragrant mix of ground spices and a gingersnap crust lend bold flavors to this cheesecake, which is a delicious change of pace at your next Thanksgiving feast. Plan ahead: the cake needs to chill overnight before serving.

1 Preheat the oven to 325°F (165°C). Wrap the outside of a 9-inch (23-cm) springform pan with aluminum foil.

2 To make the crust, in a large bowl, stir together the cookies, walnuts, granulated sugar, and butter. Pour the mixture into the springform pan. Using your fingertips, press the mixture into the bottom of the pan and about 1½ inches (4 cm) up the sides. The edges will be slightly irregular. Bake until lightly browned, about 15 minutes. Let cool slightly on a wire rack, then refrigerate until completely cool, about 15 minutes.

3 Bring a kettle of water to a boil. To make the filling, using an electric mixer, beat together the cream cheese and brown sugar on medium speed until well blended, 3–5 minutes. Add the eggs 1 at a time, beating well after each addition. Continue to beat until the mixture is smooth, about 3 minutes. Set aside ¼ cup (2 fl oz/60 ml) of the cream cheese mixture.

4 In a large bowl, stir together the pumpkin purée, cream, cinnamon, ginger, and nutmeg until well blended, about 2 minutes. Add the larger portion of the cream cheese mixture to the pumpkin mixture and beat with a mixer until well blended, about 2 minutes.

5 Pour the filling into the crust, then pour the reserved cream cheese mixture into the center. With the tip of a butter knife, swirl the mixture gently in a circular motion to make a pattern on the surface. Fill a baking pan with hot water from the kettle to a depth of 1 inch (2.5 cm) and carefully place the springform pan in it.

6 Bake until only the center barely jiggles when the springform pan is shaken, about 50 minutes. Remove the cheesecake from the baking pan and let cool on a wire rack to room temperature, about 1 hour. Cover and refrigerate for at least 8 hours or up to 1 day.

7 To serve, run a knife around the inside of the pan and then release the sides, leaving the bottom of the pan in place. Serve chilled, cut into wedges.

fresh cranberry scones

MAKES 10–12 SCONES

1½ cups (7½ oz/235 g)
all-purpose flour

1½ tablespoons sugar, plus
more for sprinkling (optional)

½ teaspoon baking powder

¼ teaspoon salt

7 tablespoons (3½ oz/105 g)
cold unsalted butter, cut
into small pieces

¼ lb (125 g) fresh cranberries

1 large egg, lightly beaten

2 tablespoons fresh
orange juice

1 egg beaten with
1 tablespoon heavy cream
(optional)

These cranberry-rich scones are so easy to make, you can put them together in the morning for a special holiday breakfast. A little bit of orange juice in the batter lends a complementary sweet-tart flavor to the scones.

1 Preheat the oven to 400°F (200°C). Have ready a large baking sheet.

2 In a large bowl, whisk together the flour, the 1½ tablespoons sugar, the baking powder, and salt. Using a pastry blender or 2 knives, cut in the butter until the mixture resembles rolled oats. Stir in the cranberries. Using a fork, mix in the egg and orange juice until a soft dough forms.

3 On a floured surface, roll out the dough into a round ½ inch (12 mm) thick. Using a 2-inch (5-cm) round cookie cutter, cut out as many rounds as possible from the dough. Gather the dough scraps, roll out again, and cut out more rounds. Place on the ungreased baking sheet. If you like, lightly brush the tops of the scones with the egg mixture and sprinkle with sugar.

4 Bake until lightly golden, about 15 minutes. Transfer the scones to a wire rack and let cool for 2–3 minutes. Serve warm.

slow-baked quinces

MAKES 4 SERVINGS

4 quinces, peeled and halved
¼ cup (2 fl oz/60 ml) dry red wine, plus more as needed
1 tablespoon sugar
Crème fraîche for serving

Quinces are tree fruits related to apples and pears that come into season in the fall. The yellow fruits have a sweet perfumelike flavor and their flesh turns a lovely pink hue when cooked. Here, they are baked in a low oven with sweetened red wine, which deepens the fruits' rosy color.

1 Preheat the oven to 325°F (165°C). Have ready a baking dish just large enough to hold the quince halves snugly.

2 Arrange the quinces cut side down in the baking dish. Add the ¼ cup (2 fl oz/60 ml) wine to the pan and sprinkle the fruits with the sugar.

3 Cover the baking dish tightly with aluminum foil and bake until the quinces are tender when pierced with the tip of a paring knife, about 4 hours, adding more wine as needed if the liquid evaporates. Let the quinces cool for about 5 minutes. Cut out the cores.

4 Serve the quinces warm in shallow bowls with some of the pan juices drizzled over the top and dollops of crème fraîche.

pumpkin pie bars

These succulent spiced bars have all the flavor you want from a pumpkin pie, but are much easier to transport to a holiday gathering and they feed a crowd easily. Be sure the pumpkin purée is very smooth before you use it. If you're short on time, you can substitute canned pumpkin purée.

For the Crust

1¼ cups (6½ oz/200 g)
all-purpose flour

1 teaspoon granulated sugar

¼ teaspoon salt

7 tablespoons (3½ oz/105 g)
cold unsalted butter, cubed,
plus butter for greasing

6 tablespoons (3 fl oz/90 ml)
ice water, plus more as needed

For the Filling

1½ cups (15 oz/470 g)
Roasted Pumpkin Purée
(page 122)

⅔ cup (5 oz/155 g) firmly
packed light brown sugar

½ cup *each* (4 fl oz/125 ml)
whole milk and heavy cream

2 large eggs, lightly beaten

1 teaspoon vanilla extract

½ teaspoon salt

2 tablespoons
all-purpose flour

1 teaspoon ground cinnamon

½ teaspoon ground ginger

⅛ teaspoon ground nutmeg

Vanilla Whipped Cream
(page 120) for serving

1 To make the crust, in a food processor, combine the flour, granulated sugar, and salt. Pulse 2 or 3 times to mix the ingredients evenly. Add the butter and pulse 8–10 times, until the butter pieces are the size of peas.

2 Add the ice water and pulse the machine 10–12 times. Stop the machine and squeeze a piece of dough. If it crumbles, add more ice water, 1 tablespoon at a time, and pulse just until the dough holds together when pinched. When the dough is ready, it should come together in a rough mass in the food processor bowl but not form a ball. Do not overmix or the crust will be tough.

3 Transfer the dough to a work surface and shape into a flat rectangle. Wrap well in plastic wrap and refrigerate for at least 1 hour or up to 24 hours, or freeze for up to 1 month.

4 Butter a 9-by-13-inch (23-by-33-cm) baking dish. On a lightly floured surface, roll out the dough into a rectangle that is slightly larger than

10 by 14 inches (25 by 35 cm) and trim the edges evenly. Transfer to the prepared baking dish and fit it into the bottom and 1 inch (2.5 cm) up the sides, being careful not to stretch or tear the dough. Refrigerate the dough for at least 20 minutes.

5 Place a rack in the lower third of the oven and preheat to 375°F (190°C).

6 To make the filling, in a large bowl, whisk together the pumpkin purée, brown sugar, milk, cream, eggs, vanilla, and salt. Sift the flour, cinnamon, ginger, and nutmeg over the mixture and whisk to combine. Pour the filling into the crust and spread evenly.

7 Bake until the filling is just set and the crust is golden brown, 35–40 minutes. Let cool on a wire rack for at least 1 hour before serving. Cut into bars and serve with whipped cream.

caramelized fig flan

3 cups (24 fl oz/750 ml) heavy cream

¾ cup (6 oz/185 g) granulated sugar

1 vanilla bean, split lengthwise

2 tablespoons unsalted butter

¼ cup (2 oz/60 g) firmly packed light brown sugar

12 Mission figs, stemmed and halved lengthwise

4 large eggs plus 4 large egg yolks

½ teaspoon salt

This take on a classic Spanish flan incorporates caramelized fresh figs that are baked in a rich egg custard. When the flan is inverted onto a platter, the figs adorn the top for a beautiful presentation.

1 In a saucepan, combine the cream, granulated sugar, and vanilla bean. Place over medium heat and bring to a gentle simmer, stirring to dissolve the sugar. Remove from the heat and let stand for 30 minutes.

2 In a frying pan, melt the butter over medium-high heat. Add the brown sugar and stir until dissolved, about 1 minute. Add the figs, cut side down, and cook until soft, about 12 minutes. Arrange the figs, cut side down, in a single layer in a round, nonstick 9-inch (23-cm) cake pan. Covering the bottom evenly with the syrup from the pan. Place in the freezer for 15 minutes.

3 Preheat the oven to 375°F (190°C). Bring a kettle of water to a boil.

4 Remove the vanilla bean pod from the cream mixture and scrape the seeds into the cream. Discard the pod. Place the pan over medium heat and bring to a simmer. Remove from the heat and cover to keep warm.

5 Whisk together the eggs, egg yolks, and salt until smooth. Slowly pour in the warm cream mixture while continuing to beat until well combined. Pour the egg mixture through a fine-mesh sieve into a bowl with a spout. Then, pour the strained mixture into the cake pan, taking care not to dislodge the figs. Place the pan in a roasting pan. Pour in hot water from the kettle to reach halfway up the sides of the cake pan. Place a sheet of aluminum foil loosely over the cake pan.

6 Bake until a knife inserted into the center of the flan comes out clean, about 40 minutes. Remove the cake pan from the roasting pan and cool on a wire rack for 2 hours. Cover and refrigerate for at least 2 hours or up to 1 day.

7 To serve, run a thin-bladed knife blade around the inside of the pan to loosen the flan. Briefly immerse the bottom of the pan in hot water to loosen the caramel. Invert a large serving plate over the top, then invert the pan and plate in a single quick motion. Lightly tap the bottom of the pan to loosen the flan, then lift off the pan. If any figs stick to the pan, use a knife tip to loosen them.

pear-walnut sticky cake

MAKES 8–10 SERVINGS

For the Cake

Unsalted butter for greasing

1 cup (5 oz/155 g) all-purpose flour, plus flour for dusting

½ teaspoon baking soda

½ teaspoon ground cinnamon

¼ teaspoon ground nutmeg

¼ teaspoon salt

¾ cup (5½ oz/170 g) firmly packed light brown sugar

5 tablespoons (2½ oz/75 g) unsalted butter, melted and cooled

2 large eggs, at room temperature

¼ cup (2 fl oz/60 ml) pear nectar

1 ripe pear, peeled, cored, and cut into ½-inch (12-mm) cubes

For the Topping

1 cup (4 oz/125 g) walnuts, toasted (page 123), cooled, and coarsely chopped

¼ cup (2 oz/60 g) firmly packed light brown sugar

4 tablespoons (2 oz/60 g) unsalted butter

1 tablespoon whole milk

For this decadent dessert, a sticky caramel-nut mixture is poured over the top of a pear-flecked butter cake. The brown sugar in the cake batter amplifies the caramel flavor, while pear nectar augments the taste of the fruit.

1 To make the cake, preheat the oven to 350°F (180°C). Butter and flour a 9-inch (23-cm) springform pan and tap out the excess flour.

2 Over a sheet of parchment paper, sift together the flour, baking soda, cinnamon, nutmeg, and salt; set aside.

3 Using an electric mixer, beat together the brown sugar, melted butter, eggs, and pear nectar on medium speed until blended, 3–5 minutes. Stir in the flour mixture just until combined and then the pear. Pour the batter into the prepared pan and spread evenly.

4 Bake until a tester inserted into the center of the cake comes out clean, about 25 minutes. Transfer the pan to a wire rack.

5 To make the topping, in a saucepan, combine the walnuts, brown sugar, butter, and milk. Place over medium-high heat and bring to a boil, stirring frequently, and then continue to boil, stirring frequently, until the mixture is reduced to a thick, saucelike consistency, about 3 minutes. Pour the hot mixture over the hot cake in the pan. Let stand for 3 minutes.

6 Release the pan sides and place the cake on a plate. Cut into wedges and serve warm.

puffy apple oven pancake

MAKES 4–6 SERVINGS

⅔ cup (3 ½ oz/105 g) all-purpose flour

2 tablespoons granulated sugar

½ teaspoon ground cinnamon

¼ teaspoon salt

4 large eggs, at room temperature

1 cup (8 fl oz/250 ml) whole milk, at room temperature

1 teaspoon vanilla extract

2 tablespoons unsalted butter, melted and cooled, plus 4 tablespoons (2 oz/60 g) butter

2 Fuji or other baking apples, peeled, cored, and each cut into 16 wedges

Confectioners' sugar for dusting

Pure maple syrup for serving (optional)

A classic oven pancake is a great addition to your brunch repertoire. Apple wedges are first sautéed and then an easy batter is poured over the top. After the pancake puffs up high in the oven, it will deflate to form an appealing, custardy texture when you remove it.

1 Preheat the oven to 425°F (220°C). Have ready an ovenproof 10-inch (25-cm) sauté pan.

2 In a small bowl, stir together the flour, granulated sugar, cinnamon, and salt. In a blender, combine the eggs, milk, vanilla, and 2 tablespoons melted butter and blend just until smooth. Add the flour mixture and blend just enough to make a smooth batter.

3 In the sauté pan, melt 3 tablespoons of the butter over medium-high heat. When the butter begins to brown, add the apples and cook, turning as needed, until golden on all sides, about 5 minutes.

Add the remaining 1 tablespoon butter and heat until it is melted and bubbling. Pour the batter over the apples and immediately transfer the pan to the oven.

4 Bake until puffed and golden, 15–20 minutes. Dust the pancake with confectioners' sugar and serve right away, directly from the pan. Pass the maple syrup at the table, if using.

cranberry-cornmeal muffins

MAKES 12 MUFFINS

1 cup (5 oz/155 g)
all-purpose flour

½ cup (2½ oz/75 g)
cornmeal

⅔ cup (5 oz/155 g) sugar

1 tablespoon baking powder

½ teaspoon salt

2 large eggs, at room
temperature

1 cup (8 fl oz/250 ml) whole
milk, at room temperature

2 tablespoons canola oil

4 tablespoons (2 oz/60 g)
unsalted butter, melted
and cooled

1 tablespoon grated
orange zest

1 tablespoon fresh
orange juice

¼ lb (125 g) fresh cranberries,
chopped

The sight of cranberries at the market heralds the holiday season, beginning with Thanksgiving in the fall. In these muffins, which incorporate cornmeal into the batter for texture, cranberries provide tart-sweet bits of color throughout. Feel free to swap in raspberries, strawberries, or blackberries for the cranberries other times of the year.

1 Preheat the oven to 400°F (200°C). Line 12 standard muffin cups with paper liners.

2 In a large bowl, whisk together the flour, cornmeal, sugar, baking powder, and salt. In a bowl, whisk together the eggs, milk, oil, melted butter, orange zest, and orange juice, then gently stir in the cranberries. Add the cranberry mixture to the flour mixture and stir just until a lumpy batter forms. Do not overmix. Spoon the batter into the prepared muffin cups, filling just to the rims.

3 Bake until a tester inserted into the center of a muffin comes out clean, 18–20 minutes. Let cool in the pan on a wire rack for about 5 minutes. Turn the muffins out of the pan and serve warm.

winter

orange butter cakes

6 tablespoons (3 oz/90 g) unsalted butter, melted and cooled, plus ½ cup (4 oz/125 g) butter, at room temperature, plus butter for greasing

2 oranges

¾ cup (6 oz/185 g) firmly packed light brown sugar

1 cup (5 oz/155 g) all-purpose flour

1 teaspoon baking powder

½ teaspoon baking soda

¼ teaspoon salt

½ cup (4 oz/125 g) granulated sugar

2 large eggs, at room temperature

¼ cup (2 fl oz/60 ml) heavy cream, at room temperature

1 teaspoon vanilla extract

Crème Anglaise (page 121) for serving (optional)

These charming individual cakes are baked in ramekins, then unmolded to reveal orange slices on the top of each dessert. The cakes are good on their own, especially served warm from the oven, but they can also be topped with a spoonful of crème anglaise for a creamy contrast.

1 Preheat the oven to 350°F (180°C). Lightly butter six 1-cup (8–fl oz/250-ml) ramekins or custard cups.

2 Finely grate the zest of 1 orange; reserve the fruit for another use. Cut the second orange into very thin slices.

3 Sprinkle 2 tablespoons of the brown sugar in the bottom of each prepared ramekin. Pour 1 tablespoon of the melted butter into each one, evenly covering the sugar. Place 1 orange slice in each ramekin. Place the ramekins on a rimmed baking sheet.

4 Sift together the flour, baking powder, baking soda, and salt over a sheet of parchment paper; set aside.

5 Using an electric mixer, beat together the ½ cup (4 oz/125 g) butter, the granulated sugar, and orange zest on medium-high speed until creamy, 3–5 minutes. Add the eggs 1 at a time, beating well after each addition. Using a rubber spatula, fold in the flour mixture. Stir in the cream and vanilla until thoroughly incorporated. Spoon the batter over the oranges in the ramekins.

6 Bake until the tops are golden and a tester inserted into the center of a cake comes out clean, about 35 minutes. Let the ramekins cool on a wire rack for 10 minutes.

7 Run a knife around the inside of the ramekins to loosen the cakes. Working with 1 cake at a time, invert a small dessert plate over the ramekin, then invert the ramekin and plate in a single quick motion. Lightly tap the bottom of the ramekin with the knife handle to loosen the cake, then lift off the ramekin. If the orange slices stick to the ramekins, use a knife tip to loosen them and replace them on the cakes. Serve the cakes warm or at room temperature with Crème Anglaise poured over the top, if desired.

pumpkin doughnuts with two toppings

MAKES 12 DOUGHNUTS

For the Doughnuts

Vegetable oil spray

2 cups (10 oz/315 g) all-purpose flour

¾ teaspoon ground cinnamon

½ teaspoon *each* ground nutmeg and ground cloves

2 teaspoons baking powder

½ teaspoon salt

¼ teaspoon baking soda

4 tablespoons (2 oz/60 g) unsalted butter, at room temperature

⅓ cup (3 oz/90 g) granulated sugar

¼ cup (2 oz/60 g) firmly packed light brown sugar

1 cup (7½ oz/235 g) Roasted Pumpkin Purée (page 122)

2 large eggs, lightly beaten, at room temperature

½ cup (4 fl oz/125 ml) buttermilk, at room temperature

For the Toppings

Maple Glaze (page 122)

¼ cup (2 oz/60 g) granulated sugar

1 teaspoon ground cinnamon

4 tablespoons (2 oz/60 g) unsalted butter, melted

Baked doughnuts are easy to make. These pumpkin ones are good both drizzled with a maple glaze and rolled in cinnamon-sugar, so we've given you both options. If you prefer just one topping, double it to make enough for all.

1 Preheat the oven to 425°F (220°C). Spray two 6-well doughnut baking pans with vegetable oil spray.

2 In a bowl, whisk together the flour, cinnamon, nutmeg, cloves, baking powder, salt, and baking soda; set aside.

3 Using an electric mixer, beat together the butter and sugars on medium speed until smooth, 3–5 minutes. Add the pumpkin purée and eggs, beating well until blended. Stir in the buttermilk. Add the flour mixture and beat until well blended.

4 Spoon the batter into a pastry bag fitted with a 1-inch (2.5-cm) plain pastry tip, or into a sealable plastic bag with one corner cut open. Pipe the batter into the prepared pans.

5 Bake until the doughnuts are golden brown and the centers spring back when touched, 8–10 minutes. Let cool in the pan on a wire rack for at least 5 minutes. Turn the doughnuts out of the pan and let cool completely on the rack, about 15 minutes.

6 To make the toppings, follow the instructions on page 122 to make the maple glaze. Set aside. In a shallow bowl, stir together the granulated sugar and cinnamon. Put the melted butter in another bowl. Using a spoon, swirl the glaze onto 6 of the doughnuts. Dip the remaining 6 doughnuts in the butter and then roll in the sugar mixture to coat evenly. Serve right away.

cranberry-pecan pie

MAKES 8 SERVINGS

**Basic Pie Dough
(page 120)**

3 large eggs

**¾ cup (6 oz/185 g) firmly
packed light brown sugar**

**½ cup (2½ oz/75 g)
light corn syrup**

**4 tablespoons (2 oz/60 g)
unsalted butter, melted
and cooled**

2 tablespoons light molasses

1 teaspoon vanilla extract

**1½ cups (6 oz/185 g) pecans,
toasted (page 123), cooled,
and coarsely chopped**

6 oz (185 g) fresh cranberries

If you are like us, you have a hard time deciding which pie to choose at the holiday buffet. This recipe offers the best of both worlds—a creative combination of classic fruit and nut pies—so you don't have to choose. If you like, cut the pie into thin slivers and set out on a platter for a holiday buffet.

1 On a lightly floured surface, roll out the dough into a 12-inch (30-cm) round about ⅛ inch (3 mm) thick. Transfer to a 9-inch (23-cm) pie pan and fit the dough into the pan (see page 117). Trim the edges, leaving a ¾-inch (2-cm) overhang. Fold the overhang under itself and crimp decoratively (see page 118). (Alternatively, reroll the scraps and cut out decorative shapes. Moisten the undersides lightly with water and place the cutouts along the pie rim.) Freeze until firm, about 20 minutes.

2 Place a rack in the lower third of the oven and preheat to 400°F (200°C).

3 In a large bowl, whisk together the eggs, brown sugar, corn syrup, melted butter, molasses, and vanilla until smooth. Stir in the pecans and cranberries. Pour the filling into the crust and spread evenly.

4 Bake until the center of the filling is set, about 45 minutes, covering the edges with aluminum foil if the crust browns too quickly. Let cool completely on a wire rack, about 2 hours, before serving.

persimmon bread pudding

MAKES 6 SERVINGS

2 tablespoons unsalted butter, at room temperature, plus butter for greasing

4–6 cups (32–48 fl oz/1–1.5 l) whole milk

1 teaspoon vanilla extract

3 large eggs, lightly beaten

½ teaspoon ground nutmeg

½ teaspoon ground cloves

1½ cups (12 oz/375 g) sugar

½ teaspoon salt

10–12 slices stale bread, each about 1 inch (2.5 cm) thick, crusts removed

1 cup (8 oz/250 g) peeled and puréed Hachiya persimmons (from 2–3 persimmons)

Vanilla ice cream, for serving

The texture of this dessert depends on the type of bread you use. Coarse-crumbed bread will easily absorb the egg mixture for a fluffy pudding. Fine-crumbed bread will yield a denser, though equally delicious, result.

1 Preheat the oven to 350°F (180°C). Lightly butter a 9-by-5-inch (23-by-13-cm) loaf pan or other baking dish.

2 If you are using fine-textured or moist bread, pour 4 cups (32 fl oz/1 l) of the milk into a large bowl; use 5–6 cups (40–48 fl oz/1.25–1.5 l) for coarse, dry bread. Add the vanilla, eggs, nutmeg, cloves, ¾ cup (6 oz/185 g) of the sugar, and the salt and whisk well. Add the bread and let stand just until it is thoroughly softened, about 2 minutes; it should not be soggy. Transfer the bread to another bowl, reserving the egg mixture.

3 Arrange a layer of soaked bread in the prepared pan. Top with one-third of the persimmon purée. Pour about one-fourth of the egg mixture over the top. Repeat twice, pushing down the layers of bread as you go. Finish with a bread layer and pour over the remaining egg mixture.

4 In a bowl, combine the butter and the remaining ¾ cup (6 oz/185 g) sugar. Using your fingertips or a wooden spoon, crumble them together and sprinkle over the top of the pudding.

5 Bake until a tester inserted into the center of the pudding comes out clean, 45–60 minutes. Let cool on a wire rack for about 10 minutes. Scoop into bowls and serve warm topped with scoops of vanilla ice cream.

pumpkin–chocolate chip mini cupcakes

**MAKES 36
MINI CUPCAKES**

1½ cups (7½ oz/235 g)
all-purpose flour

2 teaspoons baking powder

½ teaspoon salt

½ teaspoon ground cinnamon

¼ teaspoon ground nutmeg

¼ teaspoon ground cloves

½ cup (4 oz/125 g) unsalted
butter, at room temperature

¾ cup (6 oz/185 g)
granulated sugar

¼ cup (2 oz/60 g) firmly
packed light brown sugar

2 large eggs, at room
temperature

¾ cup (5¼ oz/160 g) Roasted
Pumpkin Purée (page 122)

¼ cup (2 fl oz/60 ml) whole
milk, at room temperature

¾ cup (4½ oz/140 g) plus
⅓ cup (2 oz/60 g) mini
semisweet chocolate chips

Pumpkin Frosting (page 121)

These irresistible pumpkin cupcakes feature mini chocolate chips in both the cake and the frosting. Fresh pumpkin purée contributes the best flavor here, but you could also used canned pumpkin purée, if you like.

1 Preheat the oven to 350°F (180°C). Line 36 miniature muffin cups with paper liners.

2 In a bowl, whisk together the flour, baking powder, salt, cinnamon, nutmeg, and cloves; set aside.

3 Using an electric mixer, beat together the butter and sugars on medium speed until smooth, 3–5 minutes. Add the eggs 1 at a time, beating well after each addition. Add the pumpkin purée and beat until well blended. Using a rubber spatula, stir in half of the flour mixture and then the milk just until blended. Add the remaining flour mixture and stir just until incorporated, adding the ¾ cup (4½ oz/140 g) chocolate chips during the last 15 seconds of stirring. Spoon the batter into the prepared muffin cups, filling each about three-fourths full.

4 Bake until the center of the cupcakes springs back when touched, 8–10 minutes. Let cool completely in the pan on a wire rack, about 30 minutes. (The cupcakes can be baked up to 1 day ahead of time.)

5 Spoon the frosting into a pastry bag fitted with a ¾-inch (2-cm) star tip and pipe on top of the cupcakes. Sprinkle each cupcake with the remaining ⅓ cup (2 oz/60 g) chocolate chips, dividing evenly. Serve right away, or refrigerate the frosted cupcakes for up to 2 hours.

pineapple upside-down skillet cake

MAKES 10 SERVINGS

¾ cup (6 oz/185 g) unsalted butter, at room temperature

1¼ cups (9½ oz/295 g) firmly packed dark brown sugar

1 small ripe pineapple, peeled, halved lengthwise, cored, and cut into slices about ½ inch (12 mm) thick

1⅔ cups (8 oz/250 g) all-purpose flour

1 teaspoon baking powder

1 teaspoon baking soda

¼ teaspoon salt

3 large eggs, at room temperature

1 teaspoon vanilla extract

⅔ cup (5 fl oz/160 ml) buttermilk, at room temperature

In this update on the traditional pineapple upside-down cake, the batter is baked in a cast-iron frying pan, which helps the cake achieve a beautiful caramelized color on the edges. A little buttermilk in the batter gives it a nice tang.

1 Preheat the oven to 350°F (180°C). Have ready a 10-inch (25-cm) cast-iron frying pan.

2 In the cast-iron pan, combine 4 tablespoons (2 oz/60 g) of the butter and ¾ cup (6 oz/185 g) of the brown sugar. Place over medium heat and cook, stirring, until the butter melts and the mixture is smooth. Remove from the heat and spread the mixture evenly over the bottom of the pan. Arrange enough pineapple slices on top of the mixture to cover in a single layer.

3 Sift together the flour, baking powder, baking soda, and salt onto a sheet of parchment paper; set aside.

4 Using an electric mixer, beat the remaining ½ cup (4 oz/125 g) butter on medium speed until light, about 1 minute. Add the remaining ½ cup (3½ oz/105 g) brown sugar and beat until fluffy, about 2 minutes. Add the eggs 1 at a time, beating well after each addition. Beat in the vanilla until well blended. Reduce the speed to low and add the flour mixture in 3 additions alternately with the buttermilk in 2 additions, starting and ending with the flour mixture. Beat just until combined. Spoon the batter over the pineapple, spreading to cover completely.

5 Bake until a tester inserted into the center of the cake comes out clean, about 40 minutes. Let cool on a wire rack for 5 minutes.

6 Invert a platter over the frying pan. Wearing oven mitts, invert the pan and platter together in a single quick motion. Lift off the pan. If any pineapple slices stick to the pan, use a knife tip to loosen them and replace them on the cake. Serve warm or at room temperature.

pumpkin moon pies with orange cream

MAKES ABOUT 15 PIES

For the Cakes

1½ cups (7½ oz/235 g) all-purpose flour

1 teaspoon baking powder

1 teaspoon baking soda

¾ teaspoon salt

½ teaspoon ground cinnamon

¼ teaspoon ground nutmeg

¼ teaspoon ground cloves

½ cup (4 oz/125 g) unsalted butter, melted and cooled

1 cup (7 oz/220 g) firmly packed light brown sugar

2 large eggs, lightly beaten, at room temperature

1 cup (7½ oz/235 g) Roasted Pumpkin Purée (page 122)

For the Filling

4 tablespoons (2 oz/60 g) unsalted butter, at room temperature

¼ lb (125 g) full-fat cream cheese, at room temperature

1 cup (4 oz/125 g) confectioners' sugar

2 teaspoons grated orange zest

Moon pies, also known as whoopie pies, are like an inverted cupcake, with cake on the outside and creamy frosting in the middle. They are a great choice for potlucks, as they transport more easily than other frosted desserts. If you like robust autumn flavors, you can double the spices in the cake for a spicier treat.

1 Preheat the oven to 350°F (180°C). Line 2 rimmed baking sheets with parchment paper.

2 To make the cakes, sift together the flour, baking powder, baking soda, salt, cinnamon, nutmeg, and cloves onto a sheet of parchment paper; set aside.

3 In a large bowl, whisk together the melted butter and brown sugar until smooth. Whisk in the eggs and pumpkin purée. Using a rubber spatula, fold in the flour mixture. Drop the batter onto the prepared baking sheets using a heaping 1 tablespoon for each one, spacing them about 1 inch (2.5 cm) apart.

4 Bake until the cakes spring back slightly when touched in the centers, 8–10 minutes. Transfer the cakes to a wire rack and let cool completely, about 20 minutes. (The cakes can be made up to 1 day ahead and stored in an airtight container.)

5 To make the filling, using an electric mixer, beat together the butter and cream cheese on medium speed until smooth, 3–5 minutes. Reduce the speed to low, add the confectioners' sugar and orange zest, and beat until blended. Raise the speed to medium-high and beat until light and fluffy, about 2 minutes.

6 To assemble, carefully turn half of the cakes over so they are flat side up. Spoon about 1 tablespoon of the filling onto each one. Place another cake, flat side down, on top and gently press together to spread the filling to the edges. Store in an airtight container for up to 4 hours before serving.

cranberry-buttermilk bundt cake

MAKES 12 SERVINGS

For the Cake

½ cup (4 oz/125 g) unsalted butter, melted and cooled, plus butter for greasing

3 cups (12 oz/375 g) cake flour

1½ teaspoons baking soda

½ teaspoon salt

1½ cups (12 oz/375 g) granulated sugar

2 large eggs, at room temperature

1 teaspoon grated lemon zest

1¼ cups (10 fl oz/310 ml) buttermilk, at room temperature

6 oz (185 g) fresh cranberries

¼ lb (125 g) dried cranberries

For the Icing (optional)

4 tablespoons (2 oz/60 g) unsalted butter

1 tablespoon fresh lemon juice

½ cup (2 oz/60 g) confectioners' sugar

½ teaspoon finely grated lemon zest

Here, both fresh and dried cranberries lend pronounced flavor to an easy-to-make Bundt cake. The flecks of red fruit throughout the cake's golden crumb make it a striking addition to a holiday buffet. An optional, lemon-scented icing drizzled over the top adds a beautiful finishing touch.

1 Preheat the oven to 350°F (180°C). Butter a standard, 10½ inch (26-cm) nonstick Bundt pan.

2 To make the cake, sift together the flour, baking soda, and salt over a sheet of parchment paper; set aside.

3 In a large bowl, whisk together the granulated sugar, melted butter, eggs, and lemon zest until well blended. Whisk in the flour mixture in 3 additions alternately with the buttermilk, starting and ending with the flour mixture. Fold in the fresh and dried cranberries. Pour the batter into the prepared pan and spread evenly.

4 Bake until a tester inserted near the center of the cake comes out clean, about 50 minutes. Let cool in the pan on a wire rack for 10 minutes. Invert the cake onto the rack and let cool completely, about 1 hour.

5 To make the icing, if using, in a small saucepan, combine the butter and lemon juice. Place over medium heat and warm, stirring, until the butter melts. Remove from the heat and let stand until cool, about 5 minutes. Add the confectioners' sugar and lemon zest and whisk vigorously until smooth and thickened, about 1 minute. Transfer the cake to a plate and drizzle the icing evenly over the cake, allowing it to run down the sides slightly. Let stand until the icing is set, about 1 hour.

6 Serve the cake right away, or cover and store at room temperature for up to 1 day.

shaker lemon pie

4 lemons

3 cups (1½ lb/750 g) plus 1 tablespoon sugar

Double recipe Basic Pie Dough (page 120), divided into 2 disks

7 large eggs

¼ teaspoon salt

2 tablespoons unsalted butter, melted and cooled

1 large egg white, lightly beaten

This sweet-tart pie has humble origins in the Shaker community. The filling is like a chunky lemon curd, with big hits of tart lemon slices and slightly bitter peels. The secret to success: slice the lemons very, very thinly.

1 Halve 2 of the lemons crosswise. Using the slicing blade of a food processor or a very sharp knife, slice them very thinly, cutting out the seeds as you go. Put the slices in a bowl. Remove the peel and pith from the remaining 2 lemons and discard. Chop the flesh finely, discarding the seeds. Add the flesh and juices to the bowl. Add the 3 cups (1½ lb/750 g) sugar and stir gently to coat evenly. Cover with plastic wrap and refrigerate overnight.

2 Place a rack in the lower third of the oven and preheat to 425°F (220°C).

3 On a lightly floured surface, roll out 1 dough disk into a 12-inch (30-cm) round about ⅛ inch (3 mm) thick. Transfer to a standard (not deep-dish) 9-inch (23-cm) pie pan and fit the dough into the pan (see page 117). Roll out the other dough disk for the top crust into the same-sized round.

4 In a small bowl, whisk the eggs until well blended, then add to the lemon mixture and stir well. Add the salt and melted butter and stir until blended. Pour the filling into the crust and spread evenly. Place the top crust over the filling and trim the edges, leaving a ¾-inch (2-cm) overhang. Fold the overhang under itself and crimp decoratively (see page 118). Cut a few steam vents in the top crust. Lightly brush the crust with the egg white, then sprinkle with the 1 tablespoon sugar.

5 Bake for 15 minutes. Reduce the oven temperature to 375°F (190°C) and continue to bake until the crust is golden brown and the center is slightly puffed and the filling barely feels like it jiggles when the pan is shaken, about 30 minutes longer, rotating the pan halfway through baking. Tent the pie with aluminum foil if the crust browns too quickly. Let cool completely on a wire rack, about 2 hours, before serving.

chocolate-banana bread pudding

MAKES 10 SERVINGS

4 tablespoons (2 oz/60 g) unsalted butter, melted and cooled, plus butter for greasing

2 large eggs

½ cup (3½ oz/105 g) firmly packed dark brown sugar

2½ cups (20 fl oz/625 ml) whole milk

2 tablespoons dark rum

1 teaspoon vanilla extract

1 teaspoon ground cinnamon

4 ripe bananas, peeled

6 oz (185 g) semisweet chocolate, chopped into ¼-inch (6-mm) pieces

4 cups (8 oz/250 g) stale cinnamon swirl, challah, or brioche bread cubes (from about 4 slices, each ¾ inch/2 cm thick)

1 cup (8 fl oz/250 ml) heavy cream

When other fruits are unavailable in the winter, turn to tropical fruits, which are available year-round from warmer climates. Here, they combine with chocolate and egg-rich bread in a comforting dessert. Coarsely chop the chocolate to make different-sized pieces that will melt into gooey pockets of chocolate throughout the pudding.

1 Preheat the oven to 325°F (165°C). Butter a 3-qt (3-l) baking dish.

2 In a large bowl, whisk together the eggs until blended. Whisk in the melted butter, brown sugar, milk, rum, vanilla, and cinnamon. Using a fork, roughly mash 1 banana into the egg mixture. Slice the remaining bananas and stir them in along with the chocolate. Add the bread cubes, stirring to evenly moisten them and distribute the banana slices and chocolate. Pour into the prepared baking dish.

3 Bake until the top is lightly browned and crusty, and the pudding is set when the pan is shaken slightly, about 50 minutes. Let cool on a wire rack for about 10 minutes. Serve warm with a pitcher of heavy cream to pour over the top.

persimmon quick bread

MAKES 1 LOAF

½ cup (4 oz/125 g) unsalted butter, at room temperature, plus butter for greasing

1½ cups (7½ oz/235 g) all-purpose flour

1 teaspoon baking soda

1 teaspoon salt

½ cup (3½ oz/105 g) firmly packed light brown sugar

½ cup (4 oz/125 g) granulated sugar

2 large eggs, at room temperature

1 teaspoon vanilla extract

½ cup (4 oz/125 g) sour cream, at room temperature

1 cup (8 oz/250 g) peeled and puréed Hachiya persimmons (from 2–3 persimmons)

If you have a persimmon tree in your yard, you know how prolific it can be around holiday time. This is a good recipe for using up the fruits. Loaves of this bread make great gifts during the gift-giving season. Wrapped tightly, the bread keeps for up to a week.

1 Preheat the oven to 350°F (180°C). Butter a 9-by-5-inch (23-by-13-cm) loaf pan.

2 In a small bowl, whisk together the flour, baking soda, and salt; set aside.

3 Using an electric mixer, beat together the butter and sugars on medium speed until fluffy, 3–5 minutes. Add the eggs 1 at a time, beating well after each addition, then add the vanilla and beat well. Reduce the speed to low, add the flour mixture, and beat until combined. Stir in the sour cream and persimmon purée. Pour the batter into the prepared pan and spread evenly.

4 Bake until a tester inserted into the center of the bread comes out clean, about 1 hour. Let cool on a wire rack for 10 minutes, then remove the bread from the pan and let cool completely on the rack, about 1 hour.

old-fashioned apple dumplings

MAKES 6 DUMPLINGS

For the Dough

2 cups (10 oz/315 g)
all-purpose flour

1 teaspoon granulated sugar

½ teaspoon salt

½ cup (4 oz/125 g) plus
2 tablespoons cold unsalted
butter, cut into cubes

½ cup (4 fl oz/125 ml)
ice water, plus more
as needed

6 sweet-tart baking apples,
such as Honey Crisp,
Pink Lady, or Granny Smith

Almond Streusel (page 120)

1 large egg beaten with
1 teaspoon water

2 cups (14 oz/440 g) firmly
packed light brown sugar

Pinch of salt

Vanilla Whipped Cream
(page 120) or crème fraîche
for serving (optional)

Here, a buttery, flaky dough cloaks sweet-tart apples stuffed with almond streusel. They are then drizzled with luscious caramel sauce and baked. Try Honeycrisp, Pink Lady, Granny Smith or other sweet-tart baking apples.

1 To make the dough, in a food processor, combine the flour, sugar, and salt. Pulse 2 or 3 times to mix the ingredients evenly. Add the butter and pulse 8–10 times, until the butter pieces are the size of peas. Add the ice water and pulse 10–12 times. Stop the machine and squeeze a dough piece. If it crumbles, add more water, 1 tablespoon at a time, and pulse just until the dough holds together when pinched. When ready, it should come together in a rough mass in the bowl but not form a ball. Do not overmix. Shape into a compact disk. Wrap well in plastic wrap and refrigerate for at least 30 minutes or up to 1 day,

2 Preheat the oven to 400°F (200°C). On a lightly floured surface, roll out the dough into a rectangle that is slightly larger than 14 by 21 inches (35 by 53 cm) and trim the edges evenly. Cut into six 7-inch (18-cm) squares. (Alternatively, divide the dough into 6 equal pieces and roll each into a 7-inch/18-cm square.)

3 Using an apple corer, core the apples and then peel. Place an apple on each square of dough. Stuff the hollow center with 2 heaping tablespoons of the

streusel. Brush the edges of each square with the egg mixture. Bring 2 opposite corners of the dough up over the apple and press together. Fold in the sides of the other 2 corners, bring the corners up over the apple, and press together. Repeat with the remaining apples, dough squares, and streusel. Place the dumplings in a 9-by-13-inch (23-by-33-cm) baking dish so they are not touching; refrigerate while you make the sauce.

4 In a saucepan, combine the brown sugar, salt, and 1¼ cups (10 fl oz/ 310 ml) water. Place over medium-high heat and bring to a boil, stirring well. Pour the sauce over the dumplings.

5 Bake, spooning the sauce over the dumplings twice during baking, until the crust is golden brown and the apples are tender, 35–40 minutes. Let the apples cool slightly, then serve warm with the sauce and dollops of whipped cream, if using.

pear-bourbon skillet crisp

MAKES 6 SERVINGS

Unsalted butter for greasing

For the Filling

6 firm, ripe pears, peeled, cored, and cut into wedges

3 tablespoons good-quality bourbon

3 tablespoons granulated sugar

3 tablespoons firmly packed light brown sugar

2 tablespoons all-purpose flour

½ teaspoon ground cinnamon (optional)

For the Topping

6 tablespoons (3 oz/90 g) unsalted butter, melted and cooled

½ teaspoon vanilla extract

¾ cup (4 oz/125 g) all-purpose flour

¾ cup (2½ oz/75 g) rolled oats

⅔ cup (5 oz/155 g) firmly packed light brown sugar

½ teaspoon salt

Vanilla ice cream for serving (optional)

Baked in a cast-iron frying pan, with a bourbon-scented pear filling and a buttery-crisp topping, this will become a go-to recipe during the cold months of the year. Choose Bartlett or Bosc pears that are ripe and give a little when pressed, but are not overly ripe.

1 Preheat the oven to 375°F (190°C). Generously butter a 10-inch (25-cm) cast-iron frying pan.

2 To make the filling, in a large bowl, stir together the pears and bourbon. Let stand for 30 minutes. In another bowl, stir together the sugars, flour, and cinnamon, if using. Add to the pear mixture and stir until evenly coated. Add the pear filling to the prepared pan.

3 To make the topping, in a bowl, stir together the melted butter and vanilla. In another bowl, using a fork, stir together the flour, oats, brown sugar, and salt. Add the butter mixture and stir until evenly blended and crumbly. Sprinkle the topping over the pears.

4 Bake until the pears are tender and bubbly, and the topping is crisp and brown, about 30 minutes. Let cool slightly before serving. Serve with scoops of ice cream, if desired.

making pie dough

A flaky crust is the hallmark of a good pie. The flakes are achieved by keeping the butter in discrete, cold bits within the dough. Once the dough reaches the oven, the bits of butter melt, giving off puffs of steam that lift the dough and create air pockets. For best results, keep all your ingredients and equipment very cold and work quickly. Also, take care not to overwork the dough, which leads to toughness.

1

FREEZE THE BUTTER for a few minutes to get it really cold. Meanwhile, put ice water in a liquid measuring cup and set aside. Put the cold butter on a cutting board and cut it in half lengthwise. Turn the butter on its side and cut it in half again. Cut the butter crosswise to make cubes.

2

IN A BOWL, STIR TOGETHER the flour and salt. Add the butter cubes to the bowl and toss with a fork to coat the butter well with the flour mixture. Using a pastry blender or two knives, cut in the butter until the mixture forms large crumbs the size of peas.

3

DRIZZLE THE ICE WATER over the flour-butter mixture and toss with the fork until the dough is evenly moist. If the dough seems too crumbly, add more ice water, a tablespoon at a time, and toss to mix. When the dough is ready, it should come together in a rough mass.

4

GATHER THE DOUGH together gently and form it into a compact disk. Wrap the disk in plastic wrap and refrigerate for at least 1 hour or up to 1 day before using. During the chilling time, the dough will become evenly moist and pliable, so that it is easy to work with.

rolling out pie or tart dough

When rolling out the dough, you want to use a light hand with the flour—use just enough to prevent the dough from sticking. To preserve the dough's flaky qualities, take care not to overwork the dough and keep it as cool as possible. Beginner dough-rollers can roll out the dough between sheets of parchment paper, which prevents the dough from sticking to the surface and makes it easier to transfer to the pan.

1

LIGHTLY FLOUR A WORK SURFACE such as a marble slab or counter top, or wooden or plastic pastry board. Unwrap the dough and put it in the center of the floured surface. Lightly dust the top of the dough and rolling pin with flour.

2

STARTING AT THE CENTER and working outward, roll the dough into a round that is about 2 inches (5 cm) larger than the pie pan (or as directed in the recipe). As you work, lift and turn the dough and re-dust it with flour, if necessary, to prevent the dough from sticking to the surface.

3

TO TRANSFER THE DOUGH TO THE PAN, carefully roll the dough around the rolling pin, then lift carefully to position it over the pie pan, tart pan, or baking sheet. Unroll the dough, easing it with your fingers into a centered position.

4

GENTLY PRESS THE DOUGH into the bottom and up the sides of the pie or tart pan. Using a paring knife, trim the dough evenly all around so that it is about ½ inch (12 mm) wider than the diameter of the pan (or as directed in the recipe).

embellishing dough edges

Whether you have made a single crust, a lattice crust, or a double crust pie—even a flat pie known as a galette, it's always nice to give the pie a decorative, finished edge. It will not only make your pie even more beautiful, but it will also help the crust stay in place during baking. You can also adorn a double-crust pie by applying dough cutouts to the top (page 122) or cutting steam vents in a decorative pattern.

1

TO EMBELLISH A PIE, starting at a spot nearest you, fold the dough edge under itself so that it is even with the pan sides. Continue around the circumference of the pan. You're aiming to create a thicker crust in this area than on the rest of the pie.

2

FOR A SIMPLE DESIGN, starting at a spot nearest you, press the tines of a fork deep into the crust to create hash marks in the dough. Continue to make hash marks all around the circumference of the pan.

3

FOR A FLUTED DESIGN, starting at a spot nearest you, hold the thumb and index finger of one hand about 1 inch (2.5 cm) apart and press them against the outer edge of the dough rim. Using your other index finger, press in from the inside edge of the dough rim through the opening. Repeat around the circumference of the pan.

4

TO PLEAT A GALETTE, starting at a spot nearest you, fold a section of the dough up and over the filling. Move to an adjacent spot and repeat the folding, forming a loose pleat where the folds meet. Continue around the circumference of the galette, leaving the filling exposed in the center.

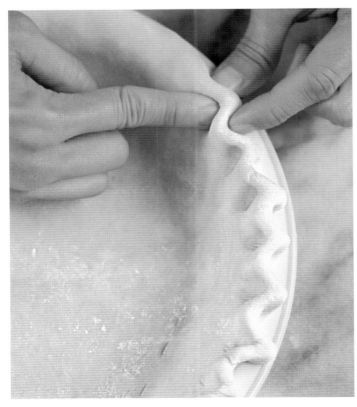

basic recipes

Basic Tart Dough

1 large egg yolk

1 teaspoon vanilla extract

2 tablespoons ice water

1¼ cups (6½ oz/200 g) all-purpose flour

¼ cup (2 oz/60 g) sugar

¼ teaspoon salt

½ cup (4 oz/125 g) cold unsalted butter, cut into cubes

In a small bowl, stir together the egg yolk, vanilla, and ice water. In a food processor, combine the flour, sugar, and salt. Pulse 2 or 3 times to mix the ingredients evenly. Add the butter and pulse 8–10 times, until the butter pieces are the size of peas.

Pour the egg mixture over the flour mixture and process just until the mixture starts to come together.

Transfer the dough to a work surface and shape into a 6-inch (15-cm) disk. Wrap well in plastic wrap and refrigerate for at least 1 hour or up to 1 day.

MAKES DOUGH FOR ONE 9½-INCH (24-CM) TART

Basic Pie Dough

1⅓ cups (7 oz/220 g) all-purpose flour

¼ teaspoon salt

½ cup (4 oz/125 g) cold unsalted butter, cut into cubes

¼ cup (2 fl oz/60 ml) ice water, plus more as needed

HAND METHOD: In a large bowl, combine the flour and salt and stir with a fork to mix evenly. Scatter the butter cubes over the flour mixture and toss with a fork to coat evenly. Using a pastry blender or 2 knives, cut in the butter until the butter pieces are the size of peas. Drizzle the ice water over the flour-butter mixture and toss with a fork until the dough is evenly moist. If the dough seems too crumbly, add more ice water, a tablespoon at a time, and toss to mix. When the dough is ready, it should come together in a rough mass. Do not overmix or the crust will be tough. Gather the dough together gently.

FOOD PROCESSOR METHOD: In a food processor, combine the flour and salt. Pulse 2 or 3 times to mix the ingredients evenly. Add the butter and pulse 8–10 times, until the butter pieces are the size of peas. Add the ice water and pulse 10–12 times. Stop the machine and squeeze a piece of dough. If it crumbles, add more ice water, 1 tablespoon at a time, and pulse just until the dough holds together when pinched. When the dough is ready, it should come together in a rough mass in the food processor bowl but not form a ball. Do not overmix or the crust will be tough.

Transfer the dough to a work surface and shape into a 6-inch (15-cm) disk. Wrap well in plastic wrap and refrigerate for at least 1 hour or up to 1 day.

MAKES DOUGH FOR ONE 9-INCH (23-CM) PIE

Almond Streusel

5 tablespoons (2½ oz/75 g) unsalted butter, melted and cooled

½ teaspoon vanilla extract

⅓ cup (2 oz/60 g) all-purpose flour

⅓ cup (1 oz/30 g) rolled oats

⅓ cup (1½ oz/45 g) chopped toasted almonds

⅓ cup (2½ oz/75 g) firmly packed light brown sugar

Pinch of salt

In a bowl, stir together the melted butter and vanilla. In another bowl, using a fork, stir together the flour, oats, almonds, brown sugar, and salt. Add the butter mixture and stir until evenly blended and crumbly.

MAKES ABOUT 1 CUP (6 OZ/185 G)

Vanilla Whipped Cream

1 cup (8 fl oz/250 ml) cold heavy cream

2 tablespoons confectioners' sugar

½ teaspoon vanilla extract

Place a deep, preferably metal mixing bowl and the whip attachment from a handheld mixer or stand mixer in the freezer until well chilled, at least 30 minutes.

Pour the cream into the chilled bowl. Fit the mixer with the whip attachment. Beat the cream on low speed until slightly thickened and little ridges are left on the surface when the whip is moved, 1–2 minutes. Slowly raise the speed to medium-high and beat, moving the whip around the bowl if using a handheld mixer, just until the cream begins to hold a very soft (drooping) peak when you stop the mixer and lift the whip, 2–3 minutes. Sprinkle the confectioners' sugar over the whipped cream and add the vanilla. Continue to beat on medium-high speed until the cream holds firm peaks that stay upright with only a slight droop when the whip is lifted, 1–2 minutes more.

If possible, serve whipped cream immediately after whipping. You can also cover the mixing bowl with plastic wrap and refrigerate for up to 1 hour. If the mixture thins or becomes a bit watery, briefly beat with the mixer or a handheld whisk.

MAKES ABOUT 2 CUPS (16 FL OZ/500 ML)

Kirsch Whipped Cream

2 cups (24 fl oz/750 ml) heavy cream

3 tablespoons confectioners' sugar

2 teaspoons vanilla extract

1½ tablespoons kirsch

In a bowl, combine the cream and confectioners' sugar. Using an electric mixer on medium-high speed, beat the mixture until soft peaks form, about 2 minutes. Whisk in the vanilla and kirsch until blended.

MAKES ABOUT 4 CUPS (32 FL OZ/1 L)

Crème Anglaise

2 large egg yolks

2 tablespoons cornstarch

5 tablespoons (2½ oz/75 g) sugar

1 cup (8 fl oz/250 ml) whole milk, heated

1 cup (8 fl oz/250 ml) heavy cream, heated

1 vanilla bean, split lengthwise

In a heavy saucepan, whisk together the egg yolks, cornstarch, and sugar until thick and pale yellow, about 2 minutes. Slowly whisk in the hot milk and cream. Add the vanilla bean and place over medium-low heat. Bring to a simmer while stirring continuously with a wooden spoon. Cook, stirring constantly, until thick enough to coat the back of the spoon, about 4 minutes.

Remove the vanilla bean halves from the cream mixture and, using the tip of a paring knife, scrape the seeds from each half in to the sauce, then stir to blend. Discard the bean halves. Use the sauce right away.

MAKES ABOUT 2 CUPS (16 FL OZ/500 ML)

Cream Cheese Frosting

1 lb (500 g) full-fat cream cheese, at room temperature

6 tablespoons (3 oz/90 g) unsalted butter, at room temperature

1¼ cups (5 oz/155 g) confectioners' sugar

1½ teaspoons vanilla extract

Using an electric mixer, beat together the cream cheese and butter on medium-high speed until smooth, 3–5 minutes. Reduce the speed to low, add the confectioners' sugar, and beat until smooth, about 2 minutes. Beat in the vanilla. Use right away.

MAKES ABOUT 2 CUPS (16 FL OZ/500 ML)

Pumpkin Frosting

6 oz (185 g) full-fat cream cheese, at room temperature

6 tablespoons (3 oz/90 g) unsalted butter, at room temperature

2–3 tablespoons Roasted Pumpkin Purée (page 122), strained to remove some of the liquid

1½ cups (6 oz/185 g) confectioners' sugar

Pinch of salt

Using an electric mixer, beat together the cream cheese and butter on medium speed until smooth, light and fluffy, 3–5 minutes. Reduce the speed to low, add the pumpkin purée, confectioners' sugar, and salt, and beat until blended. Use right away.

MAKES FROSTING FOR 36 MINIATURE CUPCAKES OR 1 DOZEN STANDARD CUPCAKES

Maple Glaze

1 tablespoon pure maple syrup

1 tablespoon unsalted butter

1 tablespoon firmly packed light brown sugar

Pinch of salt

3 tablespoons confectioners' sugar

In a microwave-safe bowl, combine the maple syrup, butter, and brown sugar. Microwave on high until the butter is melted and the mixture is bubbling, 15–30 seconds. Whisk in the salt and confectioners' sugar until smooth. Use right away.

MAKES GLAZE FOR 6 DOUGHNUTS

Roasted Pumpkin Purée

1 sugar pie pumpkin, about 2 lb (1 kg)

Preheat the oven to 350°F (180°C).

Place the pumpkin on a baking sheet. Using a paring knife, cut several slits into the flesh all around pumpkin.

Roast until the flesh pulls away from the skin, about 1 hour.

When the pumpkin is cool enough to handle, cut it in half, scoop out the seeds, and discard. Scoop the flesh into a blender or food processor and process to a smooth purée.

MAKES ABOUT 2 CUPS (15 OZ/470 G)

Fresh Cherry Filling and Syrup

1 lb (500 g) fresh Bing cherries, pitted

2 tablespoons granulated sugar

2 tablespoons kirsch

In a saucepan, combine the cherries, sugar, and ½ cup (4 fl oz/125 ml) water. Place over medium heat and cook, stirring, until the sugar dissolves. Cover and simmer for 10 minutes. Remove from the heat and drain, reserving the syrup and cherries separately. Stir the kirsch into the syrup.

MAKES ABOUT 2 CUPS (16 OZ/500 G)

basic techniques

Baking pie and tart shells

Preheat the oven to 400°F (200°C). Line the crust with heavy duty aluminum foil, making sure to press the foil into the corners or fluted edges of the crust. Fill the foil-lined crust with dried beans, uncooked rice, or pie weights.

Bake the lined crust until it dries out, about 15 minutes. Check to see if the crust is ready by pulling up one corner of the foil. If the foil sticks, the crust is not fully dried out. Return it to the oven and check every 2 minutes. Carefully remove the weights and foil.

FOR A PARTIALLY BAKED CRUST, continue to bake until the crust is lightly browned on the edges, about 5 minutes longer. Transfer to a wire rack. Use as directed in the recipe.

FOR A FULLY BAKED CRUST, continue to bake until the crust is golden brown, about 10 minutes longer. Transfer the crust to a wire rack and use as directed in the recipe.

Applying dough cut-outs on pies

Using a small cookie cutter, or working free hand with a paring knife, cut out shapes from rolled-out dough scraps. Use the back of a paring knife to add details. Affix the shapes to the top of a double-crust pie with egg wash (1 egg beaten with 1 tablespoon water) before baking.

Shaving chocolate

Using a vegetable peeler, cut thin, flat shavings from a large chunk of chocolate, letting the shavings fall onto a piece of parchment paper or plate.

Chopping chocolate

Start with a block of chocolate. Using a serrated knife, gradually cut the chocolate across the block to create even-sized pieces. Aim to make the pieces about the same size so they melt evenly.

Melting chocolate

Select a heatproof bowl that fits securely on the rim of a saucepan. Fill the saucepan with water to a depth of about 1½ inches (4 cm) and warm the water over low heat until it barely simmers. Put chopped chocolate in the bowl, taking care that it does not come in contact with any moisture. Place the bowl on the saucepan, being sure that it does not touch the water below. Heat, stirring the chocolate often (or constantly if using white chocolate) with a rubber spatula until the chocolate melts. Adjust the heat as necessary to keep the water just below a simmer. Remove the top pan or bowl from over the water and set aside to cool slightly before using.

Working with vanilla beans

Hold the vanilla bean pod in place with one hand. Using a paring knife, carefully cut down the center of the bean lengthwise. Using the tip of the knife, scrape the vanilla seeds from the inside of each pod half. The seeds will stick, so you may need to scrape twice to reach all the seeds.

Toasting nuts

Preheat the oven to 350°F (180°C). Spread the nuts on a baking sheet. Place the nuts in the oven and bake until lightly toasted and fragrant, about 10 minutes. Pour the nuts onto a plate or work surface and let cool before chopping.

Filling a pastry bag

Firmly push the desired decorating tip into the small hole in the bag. Using both hands, fold down the top of the bag to form a wide cuff. Place one hand under the cuff. Using a silicone spatula, scoop the filling or frosting mixture into the large opening in the bag, filling it no more than half full. Unfold the cuff. Push the filling or frosting down toward the tip, forcing out any air at the same time. Twist the bag several times at the location where the filling ends.

Separating eggs

Eggs are easiest to separate when they are cold. Have ready 3 clean, grease-free bowls. Crack the side of the egg sharply on a flat surface. Hold the cracked egg over and empty bowl and carefully pull the shell apart, letting the white (but not the yolk) start to drop into the bowl below. Transfer the yolk back and forth from one shell half to the other, letting the remaining egg white fall into the bowl below. Be careful not to break the yolk on a sharp shell edge. Gently drop the yolk into the second bowl. Keeping the whites free of any yolk is key if you plan to ship the whites. If the egg separates cleanly, pour the white into the third bowl. To avoid mishaps, bread each new egg over the first empty bowl and transfer the whites each time.

Working with berries and grapes

Rinse berries just before using and drain well. Rinsing them too soon could cause mold to form.

Hulling strawberries

Using your thumb to push back the stem leaves, if present. Insert a paring knife at an angle into the strawberry flesh near the stem until it reaches the middle of the top part of the berry. Place the thumb of the hand holding the knife on top of the stem and make a circular cut to release the hull and stem.

Working with rhubarb

Be sure to remove and discard any leaves from the rhubarb stalks, as they are toxic. Rinse the stalks well, then use a chef's knife to cut into pieces.

Pitting cherries

If you are using a paring knife, follow the directions for pitting stone fruits. If you are using a cherry pitter, pull off the stem. Position a cherry, stemmed side up, in the cradle of a cherry pitter. Hold the pitter over a small bowl and press down, ejecting the pit into the bowl.

Peeling peaches

Bring a large saucepan three-fourths full of water to a boil. Working in batches, immerse the peaches in the boiling water for 30 seconds, then transfer to a cutting board. When cool enough to handle, slip off the skins using a paring knife.

Pitting stone fruits

Using a paring knife, cut the fruit in half lengthwise, cutting carefully around the pit at the center. Rotate the halves in opposite directions to separate them. Use the tip of the knife to gently dig under the pit and ease it out. If the pits are too difficult to remove this way (as with clingstone fruit), use the knife to carefully carve away the flesh to release the pit.

Working with figs

Figs should be harvested when fully ripened, so look for plump, soft fruits that do not give off a milky substance when the stem is broken. Use figs as soon as possible after purchasing, storing them for no longer than 1 day in the refrigerator. Wash the figs just before using.

Peeling and coring apples

Using a vegetable peeler, starting from the stem end, remove the peel from the apple flesh in a circular motion. Cut the peeled apple in half from stem to blossom end. Turn the halves flat side down and cut them in half again to make quarters. Using a paring knife, make an angled incision into the center on one side of the core. Turn the quarter and make another incision to complete the V cut and release the core. Repeat with the remaining quarters.

To core a whole apple, hold the fruit firmly and push the corer straight down through the apple. It may take a little muscle.

Peeling and coring pears

Holding the pear at a slight angle and starting at the stem end, use a vegetable peeler to remove a strip of the peel from the pear. Rotate and repeat to remove the rest of the peel. A peeled pear can be slippery, so make sure you stabilize it on the cutting board with one hand. Using a chef's knife, cut the pear in half lengthwise. Use a melon baler to scoop the seeds form a pear half. Next, use the melon baller to create a shallow channel from the core to the stem. Repeat with the remaining pear.

Working with persimmons

There are two types of persimmons, the Hachiya and the Fuyu. Hachiya persimmons are large and acorn shaped, with a pointed end. They are the best for baking, but they need to be ripened until meltingly soft in order to rid them of their natural potent astringency. Fuyu persimmons have a smaller, rounder shape, and are better for eating out of hand. Peel hachiya persimmons before puréeing.

Working with quinces

Although edible, the peel of a quince can be somewhat bitter, so it is often removed before cooking. The firm flesh can be difficult to cut; you may need a hefty cleaver and an extra bit of effort and care to cut the fruit open. To core a quince, follow the instructions for coring apples, or cut out the softened core after cooking.

Working with pineapple

Using a serrated knife, cut off the top (crown) and bottom from the pineapple. Stand the pineapple upright on a cutting board and slice off the skin in long strips, following the curve of the pineapple and leaving the small, brown "eyes." Lay the pineapple on its side and, using a paring knife, cut away the brown "eyes" by inserting the knife at an angle and cutting around the eye until it comes free. Repeat to remove all the eyes. Using a long knife, cut the fruit in half lengthwise, then slice it crosswise into slices. Working with one slice at a time, us a paring knife to remove the tough, semicircular core sections.

index

weldonowen

1045 Sansome Street, Suite 100, San Francisco, CA 94111

www.weldonowen.com

Luscious Fruit Desserts

Conceived and produced by Weldon Owen, Inc.
In collaboration with Williams-Sonoma, Inc.
3250 Van Ness Avenue, San Francisco, CA 94109

A WELDON OWEN PRODUCTION

Printed and bound in China by 1010 Printing, Ltd.

First printed in 2015
10 9 8 7 6 5 4 3 2 1

Library of Congress Cataloging-in-Publication
data is available

ISBN 13: 978-1-61628-933-1
ISBN 10: 1-61628-933-3

Weldon Owen is a division of
BONNIER

Weldon Owen, Inc

President & Publisher Roger Shaw
SVP, Sales & Marketing Amy Kaneko
Finance Manager Philip Paulick

Associate Publisher Jennifer Newens
Associate Editor Emma Rudolph

Creative Director Kelly Booth
Art Director Marisa Kwek
Senior Production Designer Rachel Lopez Metzger

Production Director Chris Hemesath
Associate Production Director Michelle Duggan

Photographer John Lee
Food Stylist Valerie Aikman-Smith
Prop Stylist Glenn Jenkins

acknowledgements

Weldon Owen wishes to thank the following people for their
generous support in producing this book: Kris Balloun, Alicia Deal, Lillian Kang,
Kim Laidlaw, Stephen Lam, Amy Machnak, Elizabeth Parson